FOR WHAT IT'S WORTH

A CALL TO
NO HOLDS
BARRED
DISCIPLESHIP

SIMON GUILLEBAUD

MONARCH
B O O K S

Oxford, UK and Grand Rapids, Michigan

First published in the UK in 2006 by Monarch Books
(a publishing imprint of Lion Hudson plc),
Mayfield House, 256 Banbury Road, Oxford OX2 7DH
Tel: +44 (0) 1865 302750   Fax: +44 (0) 1865 302757
Email: monarch@lionhudson.com
www.lionhudson.com

Reprinted 2006.

Distributed by:
UK: Marston Book Services Ltd, PO Box 269,
Abingdon, Oxon OX14 4YN.
USA: Kregel Publications, PO Box 2607,
Grand Rapids, Michigan 49501.

ISBN-13: 978-1-85424-760-5 (UK)
ISBN-10: 1-85424-760-3 (UK)
ISBN-13: 978-0-8254-6123-1 (USA)
ISBN-10: 0-8254-6123-5 (USA)

British Library Cataloguing Data
A catalogue record for this book is available from the British Library.

Printed and bound in Great Britain by Cox & Wyman Ltd, Reading.

Contents

It has not proved possible to identify every quotation used, as much of the text was prepared under difficult conditions. If any quotation is incorrectly or inadequately attributed, please inform Monarch for correction in subsequent printings.

Acknowledgements

There are a whole load of people I want to thank for their contribution in shaping my life, let alone this book. First there were the faithful teachers at school who ran Bible studies and a weekly meeting: Mark Greenstock, James Baron, Rob Collins, David Baines. Then there was the whole Iwerne gang at many Easter and summer camps who provided solid foundations to my faith. David Jackman and his team at Cornhill imparted further tools for understanding the Bible and preaching clearly. Jeremy Crossley's pastoral heart, prayerful concern and words of wisdom were invaluable. I can't overstate my gratitude to Robert de Berry. He is the human reason why I am where I am. Thanks for responding to the Lord's prompting, and getting me out to Burundi. The result has been literally tens of thousands of lives impacted, and I praise God for Rob's speaking into my life. Some key connections and friendships which have developed along the way and led to great opportunities: Tim and Hils Grew, Mark Bailey, Mark Melluish, Alan Kilpatrick, Steve Wood, Tim Winkler, Mal Calladine, Trey Mamo, Jodi Felty, thanks for opening doors, and helping me get the message out. Diary guys, you have been a huge support, so thank you Tom Smiley, Mark Harris, Dirk Paterson, David Marfleet, Craig Riley, Ed Walker, Rob Sturgess and Simon Fowler. Simon F. and Debs Paterson, I appreciate your comments and re-shaping of the manuscript, and hopefully it's a lot better because of you. Then there are loads of people I could name in Burundi, but here are just a few: Freddie Tuyizere, my Burundian soul mate, isn't it great that we're still alive and living flat out for Him?! Onesphore Manirakiza, you lift my spirits every time I get discouraged out here; the whole team at Scripture Union, I love you, I love the closeness which we share through many dangerous shared experiences all over your beautiful country; Juergen and Monika Wiegel, Alli 'Mbabazi' Blair, Dan and Tambry Brose, for providing me (and then us) with lots of laughs and a home. Pat Symons, your brilliant efficiency as GLO administrator takes a lot off me, you're a star. Tony Collins, I appreciate you for prodding me and getting me to finish this book. Dirk, thanks for the foreword, and for constantly challenging me to resist settling for less than the best. David and Rosemary, thanks for making that third baby, and for all your support - you are great in-laws! Tracy and James, Rebecca and Katy, I love you, albeit often from a distance, you are precious siblings. Dad, I don't take for granted your releasing me, endorsing what I do, and support at every stage of my life. Thank you, you are a wonderful and generous man. Mum, thanks for modelling a beautiful life like no-one else, you are my deepest influence in pointing me in Jesus' direction. And lastly Lizzie: finally I found a lady crazy enough to join me in this extraordinary adventure of living that we have been called to. Every day is a gift. Thanks for finding my jokes funny, daring to team up with me, and adding a whole new dimension to my life on so many levels, not least with precious little Zac.

Foreword

It is rare that you come across a really authentic life. Authenticity in the Christian walk is sadly a niche quality. Most of us would say we are slightly hypocritical, don't quite live up to the game we talk. Most of us settle for *an aspiration to*, rather than *live in* the fruit of the gospel.

Not so for Simon. Through the years I have argued, challenged and prayed with him, I have found him to be a man of complete authenticity. The drive and determination I have seen in him has sometimes been frustrating as a friend, but the gospel fruit of it is hard to challenge.

If you have ever worked in the cut and thrust of the business world as I do, you will recognize that Simon is like a ruthless entrepreneur. His market is souls, and his reward, the kingdom of God. With Simon it's focus, focus, focus. Nothing gets in the way of the pursuit of salvation for the lost, his mind whirs with ideas which will allow the empire of the King to expand. Like a CEO of a global multinational he motivates, manages, cajoles and inspires his fellow workers to deliver more and more. It is never enough for Simon, always more to do. He is constantly strategizing, thinking about plans to maximise the prize.

Exhausted? Don't be. This is a book that is thrillingly illustrative of a committed life, bravely honest about its own short comings and inspiring even for the most cynical of us. Simon has an honest passion for Jesus and for the broken country of Burundi. He has an inexhaustible belief that the gospel holds the answer and his ability to communicate with wit, clarity and refreshingly without cliché cannot fail but motivate the reader.

Read this if you dare. If you are human you will laugh, cry and get on your knees. Yes, and maybe you, like me, will even be stirred to a life with greater authenticity.

Dirk Paterson
Lansons Communications
2006

Preface

For what it's worth is the offshoot of another book written several years ago, which is no longer appropriate to consider publishing. It may sound rather melodramatic, but at the time I thought death was imminent; and even if only for the sake of my limited circle of family and friends, I wanted to write about life in war-torn Burundi, Central Africa, to cover my bases! Maybe someone who dies for their faith has earned the respect and right to be listened to, I reasoned. And if the book was any good, it could have been used in some small way to contribute to the process of stirring up a new generation of passionate and reckless disciples willing to lay down their lives to see the transformation of our world.

I was in my mid-twenties, energetic, adventurous, free-spirited, and excited about living. I was a single man, and willing to consider myself more expendable than others in pursuit of dangerous dreams. I look back over the last seven years to some truly incredible times – raw, desperate, tragic, hilarious, exciting, exhilarating, fruitful and hair-raising. And I didn't die! I reached my thirties. I got married to a wonderful woman. I became a father. I'm still here! But people were on my back about writing, and maybe they were right that what I (and some of the amazing people I work with) have experienced could be shared with a wider audience to encourage and challenge fellow strugglers and stragglers to live lives of radical and passionate surrender to Jesus. Even with the best will in the world, there's always the tainted desire for people to accept, endorse and respect you. I wrestle with and admit that upfront, and have tried in the following pages to resist the temptation to paint myself in brighter colours than are warranted.

So this call to no holds barred discipleship is an amalgam of my own experiences, the experiences of a number of my heroes of the faith, and many wise words of men and women who have gone before us. I love the power of words – I often read and re-read extracts of wisdom literature which penetrate me to the core of my being – and so I hope that using a proliferation of quotes doesn't interrupt the flow or lessen the potency of the message – because the message is most certainly potent; and it needs to be if it's to contribute to the reclaiming of a dynamic, thoughtful, cutting-edge, relevant gospel to raise the bar and help arrest the decline of both the quality and quantity of those who purport to follow the Lord Jesus Christ in the Western world. That's my aim, and if I can play a small part in such a process, I'll be satisfied.

As I write this, having now finished the manuscript, Burundi is looking as good as it has done in decades. We're praying for lasting peace.

I'm always happy when I come to the end of reading a book if I can pick out a couple of gems that deeply hit home and challenged or impacted my outlook and behaviour. Here's hoping something smacks you in the face and leaves you reeling and re-envisioned with an irresistible desire to live and love both God and people with all your heart, mind, soul and strength.

God bless you. *Soli Gloria Deo.*

Simon Guillebaud
May 2006

Introduction

This book on no holds barred discipleship is a call to radical living. It's not in any way about going to Burundi – I simply include personal experiences throughout this book to validate what I say so that you know at least a little about where I'm coming from. Neither is radical living about having to leave your country of origin to go and serve God overseas, nor transforming overnight into a zealous extremist. It's rather about living our lives to the full, maximizing all our gifts for God's glory, seeking to exhibit and demonstrate an authentic biblical Christianity, and completely embracing the adventure of living.

In December 1999, I wrote the following during a lonely and sleepless night in Africa:

I so long to be used to awaken a passion in people's hearts for radical living. We are all just ordinary people, with the potential to do extraordinary things because we have an extraordinary God.

Some nights I lie awake consumed with excitement at the task in hand, ideas whirling around my head, huge dreams to see nations turning to Christ, frustrated about how many of us can talk a good game but are not prepared to pay the price to deliver the goods. God has blessed me with times of unbelievable intimacy, where I've wept with love for him, joy in him, desperation for friends and family who are currently rejecting him. How can they miss out on this? It's so real, so big, so important. I must give all, not just most, but all...

13

However tonight I'm awake not because of joy – rather a mixture of emotions caused by reading about the suffering church, untold nameless faceless "unpeople" who are my brothers and sisters, not in the flesh but so much deeper than that. Raped, imprisoned, tortured, humiliated, traumatized, murdered. And it's happening *right now* as I lie here comfortably in bed, warm, cosy, a roof over my head, food in my belly, secure with family and loved ones, knowing there's freedom of speech, freedom of religion. Did I use that freedom today? Ruel Janda had his head chopped off in a Saudi jail for reading the Bible – he was only there in the first place under fabricated charges.

God, what's happening? What are we doing? Forgive my lukewarmness.

Many of our brothers and sisters around the world understand far better than I do what answering obediently to the call of Christ entails. The following pages are an exploration, a challenge and a rebuke to myself as much as to anyone else. We're all "work-in-progress" and have a long way to go, and I write in humility, still far from the finished article. I've divided it into three parts, so that we know where we're going. Part One asks *how* I can live radically, Part Two asks *why* I might want to live radically, and Part Three investigates *what* radical living will look like.

God calls people in many different ways, to all sorts of different vocations. He longs to harness the gifts he's given us to be used in his service. We're all unique, which means we all have a unique blend of character strengths and weaknesses, of gifts and foibles. We can never be prescriptive about how God calls, or what area of work is more significant or strategic for his kingdom. The crucial factor is simply to recognize that he calls all of us to full surrender.

In my case, this life of surrender has taken me to Central Africa over the last seven years. With varying degrees of intensity, that has meant living in a war zone, and so life has been far from ordinary – at least for those who haven't lived through a time of war. Not many of us would consider it normal, for example, to have had an armed robbery a couple of houses down, a rocket fired between the cars of two friends, nights of intense shelling over the capital, and my flatmate's health centre trashed by rebels. Yet all those events happened in the space of seven days – and a prominent and influential friend was assassinated immediately before. So this kind of life isn't remotely ordinary for most readers, although unfortunately it's been business as usual for years for the largely forgotten people in the heart of Africa.

When you live in a war zone, you think regularly about dying. Out here we see death, we hear about death, we are regularly confronted by death. It focuses my mind on what really matters. It refines and defines my priorities. It puts into context my petty obsessions. And so the prospect of imminent death can have a very positive impact on my life. I don't dwell on it, but it's always there in the shadows.

Yet although not many people live in such extreme circumstances, and we may not be living in a literal war zone, *all of us are involved in a spiritual war zone.* You and I need to recognize that there's a battle going on for our hearts. What I watch, what I listen to, what I spend my time and money on – all those things have an impact on my heart. The insidious impact of advertising, the media, magazines, and popular culture, which define me on such shallow

criteria as how I look, who I know, what I wear, eat or drive
– all these erode my true sense of identify and worth as a
child of God, and dilute my passion for what has real value
and substance. Our guard is so often down. We seldom protect our hearts. We let almost anything in. Where is the vigilance, the discernment, the scrutiny? Our hearts are far too
precious to treat with such lax indifference. Solomon himself as king of Israel emphasized this point, advising,
"Above all else, guard your heart, for it is the wellspring of
life" (Proverbs 4:23).

The message of this book is that God wants our everything – not to limit us or stop us enjoying life – rather to
release us in his appointed calling. It's a radical and
straightforward message, but one which is seemingly so difficult to embrace. Yet if he gave everything for me, and
knows what's best for me, then surely it makes sense giving
it all back to him to use for his purposes and for his glory.

Most of us will admit, perhaps ruefully, that our lives
don't match up to the words we profess to believe. The
temptation is to shrug our shoulders and resign ourselves to
spiritual mediocrity. But if we do that, the result for our
personal lives and for society as a whole is disastrous.
Having been called by Jesus to act as preserving salt, we end
up acquiescing to the insidious erosion of societal values.
Having been called by Jesus to act as piercing and reflecting
light, we prefer to merge into the shadows. Consequently
our impact is largely nullified. Perhaps legitimately
Nietzsche reproached the Christians of his day for "not
looking like they were saved". Guinness provides this more
contemporary scathing indictment: "In the decades I have
followed Jesus, second only to the joy of knowing him has
been a sorrow at the condition of those of us today who

name ourselves his followers. If so many of us profess to live by the gospel yet are so pathetically marginal to the life of our societies and so nondescript and inconsequential in our individual lives, is there something wrong with the gospel, or does the problem lie with us?"

Faced with such a bleak analysis, we can choose the road of sanctified resignation, or we can bite back angrily. However, as I've preached in dozens of churches in Europe and North America, as well as at schools and on campuses, I almost always come across individuals or groups who are passionate to give God their all. Maybe you're one of them. I hope so. If not yet, may it be the case by the end of our journey together in these pages.

In a way, we're victims of the fact that there are so few role models nowadays to show us how it's done; or rather, there are so few role models whom we can relate to in the Western church. Plenty of brothers and sisters in the persecuted and suffering church are living out a radical expression of Christianity, but their circumstances are so far removed from our own context that we find them harder to relate or aspire to. It's been my privilege to observe and work alongside a number of beautifully radical followers of Christ, who have modelled to me the life of costly faith, endurance and adventure. Their daily experience is so different from our rebranded Western Christianity, which has mostly lost its cutting edge and vitality. We've much to learn from them, if we're ready to draw humbly alongside them and listen to the penetrating insights gained in the crucible of suffering.

One of our biggest problems has arisen out of the privatization of our faith. The result of a privatized faith is that Christ's lordship is restricted to certain times and places in our compartmentalized lives. We may hang him on the coat peg with our jacket as we enter the office, or in the locker in the changing room before training on the team, and only pick him up at the end of the day's work or after the training session. People aren't attracted by the hypocrisy of Sunday religion; they want the reality of a consistent and dynamic 24-7 relationship which transcends the suffocating pressures and ambitions of day-to-day existence. Often our problem doesn't lie in the fact that we're in the wrong place – rather we're not living out the reality of our faith where we are.

How can we make sure we are what we should be where we are? We need to immerse ourselves afresh in the Scriptures, to be struck anew by the all-encompassing nature of Christ's call on the original disciples' lives – a call which must similarly envelop, infuse and impact our own lives two millennia later. We need to reject the diluted gospel we have unwittingly imbibed. Following Jesus isn't about being respectable or nice. No, as we accept Christ's call, something far more powerful and dangerous is unleashed in our lives. Jesus wants to turn us into wide-eyed radicals. If being "nice" is our highest aspiration, the gospel is emasculated and becomes simply life-*enhancing* instead of life-*transforming*. Nice people are never offensive, and yet at some stage the gospel must offend, because it highlights areas of inconsistency and hypocrisy in my own life, as well as in the lives of those who reject Jesus for who he claims to be. If our greatest virtue is that we don't offend anyone, then there will be no potency or passion in our message or movement, which ends up being okay news instead of the best news in the world.

Every day in almost every situation the temptation for

me is to settle for less – and I guess it's the same for you. To resist such temptation, we need the deep reverential worship of the Father, the liberating grace of the Son, and the enabling power of the Holy Spirit as we choose to live and give, in Oswald Chambers' words, our "utmost for his highest". For that's what he's worth.

Part One:

No Holds Barred Discipleship –
How can I live radically?

CHAPTER ONE

Risky Business

Having been approached back in 1998 about going to work as an evangelist in Burundi, I ended my marketing job and prepared to leave family, friends, financial security, and all that was familiar to me. It was time to take some radical risks. But just a few days before my departure date, the same man who had recruited me rang up and apologized – the church in Burundi didn't want an evangelist after all, but an administrator. He was sorry, but unfortunately that would be my expected role. What?! I hung up the phone in confusion and disbelief. Lord, what's going on? Have I got it wrong? Is this a huge mistake? But it was too late. I had bought my ticket, said farewells, and was ready to go. I was risking a great deal, and maybe would end up looking a complete idiot if things didn't work out, but I truly believed the Lord had called me to Burundi, and so to refuse would have been an act of disobedience.

First of all I flew to Rwanda to spend four months with my feisty aunt and grandmother, who were both working in the north of the country. Granny was extremely hardcore, and she was going to be my language teacher. She had been in Rwanda for half a century, and the languages of Rwanda and Burundi are similar, so for those four months I studied the language and pleaded with the Lord to release me from the job as administrator. I wanted to work for Scripture Union in Burundi, because SU works with youth and is interdenominational. Meantime the team of workers themselves at SU in Burundi heard that a *muzungu* (a white man) was coming down in a few months and wanted to join them. So they began praying along the same lines. Those prayers went on over the next few months, until on my second last night in Rwanda, Granny prayed me off with the words: "Lord, Simon's surrendered to you. We've had enough of him! If you want to humble or teach him something in making him an administrative assistant, then so be it. We just ask that you'll overrule and make it clear."

I said goodbyes to all my friends in that town and headed for the capital, Kigali. Arriving in Kigali, I went to a guesthouse to meet my boss who had flown out from the UK. I stopped by for ten minutes, when we were amazed to discover that the head of SU Burundi had also just arrived on his way to Tanzania. Surely not! Here were three men from three different countries in transit to two different countries, who were praying for the same thing, and whose paths had crossed at the exact time necessary in that one specific guesthouse in the whole of the capital city. We praised the Lord, seeing his hand clearly at work, committed it to him, and then I drove off to a friend's house for my last night in Rwanda, thrilled with the anticipation of how God would continue to intervene to free me up to work for SU.

The reality was that I was still lined up for a job in a totally foreign and alien country at war, and for work which I wasn't skilled at and didn't want to do. I knew virtually nobody, possessed just a few hundred dollars, had given up everything, and had no idea how things would turn out. But in the midst of such precariousness and uncertainty, I experienced a nervous peace. I had peace, because I knew God had to be faithful; and it was a nervous peace, because things were totally out of my hands yet I knew something significant was about to happen. I had risked my all and surrendered everything to him, so I knew he would be faithful and honour my trust in him.

As we crossed the border into Burundi the following day and came down through the mountains, I caught sight of Bujumbura nestled below in the plain next to Lake Tanganyika, with a mesmerizing sunset melting over the Congolese peaks beyond. It was breathtaking. This was my new home for the foreseeable future. I was utterly vulnerable and at the mercy of forces beyond my control. What a wonderful position of complete dependence and weakness to be in to see the hand of God at work! My diary records, "20th January 1999: This is my new home – for one year? Two years? Ten? Fifty? *Bizi Imana*, God knows. Full of excitement, tired, nervous, exhilarated. It's so beautiful – but what a mess…"

I immediately found an internet café, and sent my first email from Burundi to friends and family, telling them how excited I was at God's leading, that he was paving the way for me to work at SU, and that SU was bankrupt and needed a computer. I sent that email off, and received a prompt reply from a civil servant friend in London who was ecstatic as he wrote, "I can't believe it, this sort of stuff never happens to me! This morning I prayed to God and told him that I wanted to give my computer to somebody, so could he show me who it was. And then I logged on and got your email asking for a computer!"

Sign after sign came to show that God was in charge. He was utterly faithful, supplying "all [my] needs according to his glorious riches in Christ Jesus" (Philippians 4:19). C. S. Lewis says, "God gives where he finds empty hands." Well,

I was empty-handed, vulnerable, weak and dependent on his mercy. In such a position, it was wonderful to observe him honouring the risks I had taken.

To risk or not to risk

Today most of us live in societies that seek to minimize risks at all costs. For a reasonable fee, we can insure ourselves against the serious consequences of most accidents or potential disasters. If our car is broken into or stolen, or our house flooded, it may cause significant inconvenience, but it doesn't lead to economic ruin as it might without the safety net of the insurance cover.

But in the domain of faith, different dynamics apply. We can't and shouldn't aspire to neatly packaged formulae or plans. The great man of faith, Hudson Taylor, made the following observation: "Unless there's an element of risk in our exploits for God, there's no need for faith." Our danger is that we may faithfully attend our respective churches, read our Bibles, contribute to the needs of the community, tick all the boxes of what a Christian is meant to do, and yet never take a single risk. Even on a business level, by and large it is the companies that take risks that are long-term successful.

That's part of the reason why following Jesus is meant to be an adventure. The journey is unpredictable, full of unexpected detours – sometimes distractions and dangers too – but we can have confidence in the One who's leading the way. He's the Good Shepherd. He looks back and asks us whether we're willing to follow him wherever he chooses to take us. Are we?

Fear of failure

Many of us are afraid of taking risks in case things don't work out well – in case we "fail". Such concerns are legitimate, but perhaps we need to reassess what constitutes "failure". Is failure when things don't work out as we had hoped or expected? Or is failure not having the courage to risk living out our dreams?

One of our most famous old boys at school was Winston Churchill. He actually hated our school and ran away, but we forgave him that and were happy to brag about him and the solid education which underpinned and helped shape this great leader! Years later, Churchill was asked by a journalist in an interview what experience had best equipped him to risk being shunted out of office as he spoke out against Hitler shortly before the latter seized control in Germany in the years leading up to the Second World War. To the interviewer's amazement, Churchill recalled the time he had been forced to repeat a year at school.

"You mean you failed a year at school?"

"I never failed anything; I was given a second opportunity to get it right."

As John Ortberg says, "Failure is not an event, but rather a judgement about an event. Failure is not something that happens to us or a label we attach to things. It is a way we think about outcomes.

Before Jonas Salk developed a vaccine for polio that finally worked, he tried 200 unsuccessful ones. Somebody asked him, "How did it feel to fail 200 times?"

"I never failed 200 times," Salk replied. "I was taught not to use the word 'failure'. I just discovered 200 ways how not to vaccinate for polio."

Were either Winston Churchill or Jonas Salk failures? Or how about Hillary? Ortberg continues, "Sir Edmund Hillary made several unsuccessful attempts at scaling Mount Everest before he finally succeeded. After one attempt he stood at the base of the giant mountain and shook his fist at it. 'I'll defeat you yet,' he said in defiance. 'Because you're as big as you're going to get – but I'm still growing.' Every time Hillary climbed, he failed. And every time he failed, he learned. And every time he learned, he grew and tried again. And one day he didn't fail."

So we embrace the fact that progress in any sphere comes through repeated attempts, "failures", followed by renewed and modified approaches. Instead of seeing apparent failures as stumbling blocks, they're transformed into stepping stones. Max Planck, Nobel Prize winner for the formulation of the quantum theory, observed, "Looking back over the long and labyrinthine path which finally led to the discovery, I'm vividly reminded of Goethe's saying that men will always be making mistakes as long as they are striving after something." Failing is not falling down, but rather staying down. There's a fresh start available after every mistake, if we get back up and fight on. It simply takes guts. As Churchill said, "Success is never final; failure is never fatal. It's courage that counts."

Mistakes and supposed failures are part of the risk of daring to live. I can stay in the same dead-end dissatisfying job for fear of being rejected at another job interview. I can distance myself from any close relationship for fear of being let down or hurt. I can embrace the status quo at all costs for fear that a rocking boat might destabilize what I've come to accept as my lot in life. But as a follower of Jesus, the call to no holds barred discipleship denounces those options. Roosevelt declared, "The person who succeeds isn't the one who holds back, fearing failure, nor the one who never fails...but rather the one who moves on in spite of failure. Far better it is to dare mighty things, to win glorious triumphs, even though checkered by failure, than to take rank with those poor spirits who neither enjoy much nor suffer much because they live in the gray twilight that knows not victory or defeat."

Leaving the safety of the harbour

We must choose freedom from our natural inclination towards safe convention and well-worn paths. We don't want to look back with regret at what could have been. Just after his college days at Cambridge, Malcolm Muggeridge scribbled his own epitaph to a fellow student: "Here lieth one whose soul sometimes burned with great longings, to whom sometimes the curtain of the Infinite was opened just a little, but who lacked the guts to make any use of it." What tragic candour!

A ship may be safe in the harbour, but to fulfil its purpose, it has to take on the seas; and no new land was ever discovered without the ship's commander agreeing to lose sight of the shore he'd embarked from. Anticipating future regret, Mark Twain warns us, "Twenty years from now you will be more disappointed by the things that you didn't do than by the ones you did do. So throw off the bowlines. Sail away from the safe harbour. Catch the trade winds in your sails. Explore. Dream. Discover."

Sailing away, catching unpredictable winds in our sails, exploring, dreaming, discovering – none of these are safe activities. In fact they're dangerous ones. But a cursory glance at the Scriptures confirms to us the assumption that following God in obedience all the way is a dangerous and costly decision. From Abraham's leaving his country, people and father's household to go to the land God would show him (Genesis 12:1), through Stephen's martyrdom, to Paul's repeated floggings and ultimate execution, to John's exile on the isle of Patmos, all recognized and accepted the potential implications of stepping out in reckless faith.

Yet the danger and risk in wholly embracing Christ's call are mitigated by countless assurances. Paul can triumphantly exclaim, "Who shall separate us from the love of Christ? Shall trouble or hardship or persecution or famine or nakedness or danger or sword?... No, in all things we are more than conquerors through him who loved us" (Romans 8:35, 37). God promises us, "Never will I leave you; never will I forsake you" (Hebrews 13:5). We're on the winning side, with victory totally assured. Paul can stand up defiantly and confront the ultimate enemy and declare, "'Death has been swallowed up in victory'... The sting of death is sin, and the power of sin is the law. But thanks be to God! He gives us the victory through our Lord Jesus Christ" (1 Corinthians 15:54–57).

Death will come to us all. But it's an emasculated enemy for those whose confidence is in the vacated cross and empty tomb. At significant moments in our lives, at key times of decision-making, our resurrection hope will enable us to leave the safety of the harbour. The aging author Brennan Manning reflected towards the end of his life that "the defining moments of my life have not been my sins or my successes. They've been a depressingly small number of decisions that involved real risk".

This is a dangerous realization which will have ramifications beyond what we could ever foresee. The Japanese kamikaze pilots were so very dangerous precisely because they didn't fear for their lives. Scott Peck wrote, "What we desperately need to re-understand is that it's dangerous to be a true Christian. Anyone who takes his or her Christianity seriously will realise that crucifixion isn't something that happened to one man two thousand years ago, nor was martyrdom just the fate of his early followers. It should be an omnipresent risk for every Christian. Christians should – need – in certain ways to live dangerously if they're to live out their faith... It's time for communal, congregational action and corporate risk."

Both individual and corporate risk will mean getting our hands dirty. Francis Schaeffer was a brilliant American apologist who took risks for himself and his young family in moving to Switzerland and reaching out to many disillusioned "enlightened" students. With his wife Edith, he founded a community called *L'Abri* (French for "Shelter"), and saw the Lord work in extraordinary ways through their surrendered lives. But it was messy, difficult, frustrating, and risky. He wrote of their experiences,

> In about the first three years of L'Abri all our wedding presents were wiped out. Our sheets were torn. Holes were burned in our rugs... Drugs came into our place. People vomited on our rugs... How many times have you had a drug-taker come into your home? Sure it's a danger to your family, and you must be careful. But have you ever risked it? ... If you've never done any of these things or things of this nature, if you've been married for years and years and had a home (or even a room) and none of

this has ever occurred, if you've been quiet especially as our culture is crumbling about us, if this is true – do you really believe that people are going to hell?

The common sense of risk-taking

A few years ago I was involved in a weekend of outreach in the bush, and had a few spare hours to myself to read and pray. It was at a time when things were particularly tense, with a number of attacks in the area. I wrote the following in my journal:

This book on C. T. Studd has been so profoundly challenging. Quite apart from working in China and India for umpteen years, having given up *all* his *massive* inheritance, and fleeing the adulation of the whole nation as the best English cricketer of his day – it's the pioneer evangelism in the heart of Africa that blows me away. What a risk-taker: ignoring what everyone told him because he knew the Lord was calling; suffering from chronic asthma and in his fifties, yet walking 700 miles through the Zairian jungle for two years surveying the needs; lasting eighteen altogether and seeing numerous tribes reached with the gospel; going without any financial security, because no society would back him; trusting the Lord to provide for every need; praying and waiting on the Lord from 3.30am each morning; translating the New Testament into the local dialect whilst on his deathbed working eighteen hours a day; seeing an indigenous mission movement commence. So many setbacks, hardships, trials, rejections.

Wow! I cannot relate to the man – he is far too hard-core for me – and yet I want to relate to him. I want to do absolutely everything for the Lord, because he is worth everything – and yet of course I want to hold on to common sense. *But the Lord does not work on the basis of common sense!* That's so clear to me. The good is the enemy of the best. Common sense will so often rational-ize averageness and lukewarmness – I shouldn't think there ever was a man or woman of God who achieved anything of note for the Lord's glory who followed the path of common sense at key decision-making times. I'm bored of people telling me to be careful, to stop taking risks, and I'm bored of being sensible or careful. I want to be recklessly effective in his service, and work by kingdom dynamics. Better go out guns a'blazing! What a God we serve! Awesome, precious, holy, risen Jesus! *Holy Spirit, I beg you to fill me! I so need your touch, anointing, empowering and leading!*

And as if to confirm the above thoughts, the reading from my daily devotional was as follows: "The simplicity that comes from our natural common sense decisions is apt to be mistaken for the witness of the Spirit, but the Spirit wit-nesses only to his own nature and to the work of Redemption, never to our own reason. If we try to make him witness to our reason, it is no wonder that we are in darkness and perplexity. Fling it all overboard, trust in God, and he will give the witness."

I realize I'm treading on dangerous ground, and opening myself up to significant misunderstanding. I'm not advocat-ing an abandoning of our critical faculties, a spontaneous embarking on ill-conceived adventures, or a jeopardizing of the safety and well-being of others. Neither am I saying that common sense is wrong, or is to be jettisoned as conflicting at all times with the life of faith. Common sense is a God-given faculty, an endowment without which we couldn't survive. However, common sense wouldn't advocate sending Jesus to the cross. Common sense would preclude adhering to or implementing much of what Jesus said. Common sense rationalizes away most of the dynamics of faith, because it operates on a different plane. That's why the message of the cross is "foolishness to those who are perishing" (1 Corinthians 1:18). It's quite simply an absurd message – unless it's a historical reality. Chambers adds, "Never let common sense obtrude and push the Son of Man to one side. Common sense is a gift which God gave to human nature; but common sense is not the gift of his Son. Supernatural sense is the gift of his Son; never enthrone common sense." Once we embrace the message of the cross as the absolute truth, then the call to no holds barred discipleship does indeed include risk-taking.

Although ignorant of our earthly future, we're certain of our eternal destination. So, clichéd as it sounds, even though we don't know what the future holds, we do know God holds the future. He's the safest gamble, because he's not a reckless gambler. He's supremely in control. As Jesus removed our eternal risk, he calls us to daily continual risk. I can take risks because he's ultimately secure. Following him may not be a safe journey, but he's the Sovereign God, and can be trusted. If he's got the whole wide world in his hands, then that includes me – and his is the safest pair of hands in the world. Risky business? Emphatically "yes"!

CHAPTER TWO

What Do You Mean?

The call to no holds barred discipleship is a call to radical living – throughout this book I am using these terms interchangeably; and whereas respectable living is playing it safe, radical living is risky business. That's clear from the last chapter. But before we go any further, what exactly do I mean by the word "radical"? Franklyn D. Roosevelt describes a radical as a "man with both feet planted firmly in the air"! Whilst obviously rejecting his quip as a working definition, we do want a clear one in order to avoid any potential misunderstanding or misinterpretation, because words like "radical", "fundamentalist" and "fanatic" come from the same stable of words with largely negative connotations. They evoke images of misguided, aggressive and destructive groups or individuals, be they from the political, ideological or religious sphere. However, the word "radical" is simply derived from *radix*, which is Latin for "root". The Oxford Dictionary describes it as "going to the root or origin; touching or acting upon what is essential or fundamental; thorough". Webster's elaborates with the idea that someone or something 'radical' is "marked by a considerable departure from the usual or traditional...disposed to make extreme changes in existing views, habits, conditions or institutions".

So we'll try to get back to the roots, origins, essentials and fundamentals of Christianity. Such a process will involve a considerable departure from what's been misrepresented to us as normal, reasonable, or traditional Christianity; and conceivably, dare I say hopefully, the result will be some extreme changes in our current views, habits, conditions, and institutions. I believe we need a complete paradigm shift to recapture the essence of what it means to be a follower of Jesus Christ.

Below are a few key clarifications.

Saying that God matters most doesn't imply that everything else matters little

Rabbi Abraham Heschel said, "God is of no importance unless he is of supreme importance." Whilst agreeing with him, we acknowledge the potential danger of such a pronouncement. Observe the skewed single-mindedness of one young Marxist: "There's one thing about which I'm dead in earnest – the communist cause. It's my life, my business, my religion, my hobby, my wife, my mistress, my bread and my meat."

Well, that's way too extreme. You can't deny the depth of conviction and commitment to his cause, but Jesus isn't asking us to adopt such blinkered and imbalanced loyalty. We don't just want to replace a single-issue Marxist fanatic (or Islamist, or secularist etc.) with a single-issue Christian fanatic. It's not the case that God matters more than everything else, so nothing else matters in the light of him. On the contrary: because God matters infinitely, everything else matters much more in the light of him.

So the environment matters immensely, because God is Creator of the world. He loves his world, is committed to it, died for it, and will ultimately re-create it. Art matters because we're made in God's image, and his creativity has been passed on to us. Justice matters, because it's an intrinsic component of God's character. That's why Christians are to be at the forefront of shaping and contributing to issues of the environment, the arts, and justice, as we seek to witness to our Creator and bring glory to him. During childhood and adolescence, through motherhood or fatherhood, as students or pensioners, in times of employment and unemployment – all provide different opportunities and settings in which to glorify God. We embrace a holistic theology which addresses every area of our lives and provides a framework from which to validate or repudiate what we're engaged in. For example, we affirm that our work matters to God. As such we see the inherent worth in our careers, as we use the gifts God has given us. This latter thought leads us to an important distinction.

The term "full-time Christian worker" is a misnomer, as all Christians are full-time

Mark Greene explains tongue-in-cheek the false construct implicitly adhered to by most of us Christians: "All Christians are born equal, but 'full-time' Christians are born more equal than others. In turn, there is an unspoken hierarchy that goes something like this: pastor, overseas missionary, full-time Christian worker, tentmaker (so long as it's abroad), elder, deacon, poor Christian, Christian, rich Christian."

He continues, "All vocations are equal, and so-called 'secular work' is a vocation. Many of our Bible heroes were in fact workers e.g. the Israelite midwives who, struggling for medical biblical ethics, boldly defied Pharaoh's command to kill all male Israelite babies [Exodus 1:15–22], Joseph the chancellor [Genesis 41:41], Daniel the imperial adviser

[Daniel 2:48], Nehemiah the security agent [Nehemiah 4:12–15]."

One cannot overestimate the insidious effect that such a misrepresentation of the validity of "secular" work has had on committed believers. Greene highlights the danger, saying that "the impact on Christians of effectively robbing their work of spiritual and ministry value is to produce a sense of guilt. The working Christian comes home at the end of a fifty-hour week and thinks, 'I haven't done any evangelism. I haven't done any ministry. I'm not serving God. I must make time outside work to do all these things, otherwise I'm not leading an obedient Christian life'. So perhaps he or she gets involved in neighbourhood evangelism, or accepts the invitation to serve on the diaconate, and tries to squeeze a hundred commitments into a seven-day week. The result can simply be exhaustion and discouragement".

Ironically, as a supposedly "full-time" Christian worker, I might conceivably be reinforcing that very error, as the almost implicit assumption could be falsely verbalized as, "If you become really keen and passionate in your faith, then you should leave your 'career' and go into the 'ministry'." N.B. That is *not* what I'm saying. Wilberforce himself nearly made this very mistake when he was converted at the age of 25 in 1785. He made the false deduction that he should shelve politics and go into the ministry, as "spiritual" affairs were far more important than "secular" affairs.

Thankfully, John Newton, the former slave trader, intervened and persuaded him to persevere in the political domain. "It is hoped and believed that the Lord has raised you up for the good of the nation," said Newton, echoing Mordecai's words to Queen Esther (Esther 4:14). After much soul-searching and seeking the Lord's guidance, Wilberforce consented and embarked on a lifelong campaign as a parliamentarian, speaking out against many of the social evils of the day and being used by God to bring about radical transformations with worldwide repercussions. He scribbled in his journal in 1788, "My walk is a public one. My business is in the world; and I must mix in the assemblies of men, or quit the post which Providence seems to have assigned me."

The Bible doesn't differentiate between the physical and spiritual parts of human life in the same way that we tend to; and God doesn't distinguish or compartmentalize "work" and "worship" – indeed the Hebrew words for both "work" and "worship" are derived from the same root. So it's not just when we praise or pray that we're doing our spiritual duty, but also when we offer up our work to the Lord. All our activities can be worship offered up to our heavenly Father. Paul wrote to the Colossians, "Whatever you do, work at it with all your hearts, as working for the Lord, not for men" (3:23). So it's not about doing "religious" things well, rather that God's influence invades the totality of our lives.

In seeking to be disciples of Jesus, our aim is to live in any and every situation as he would live if he were us. It's not *what* I do, but *how* I do it. Otherwise, if my job isn't a supposedly "full-time" one, then I'll be spending a large proportion of my waking hours excluding Jesus' relevance and primacy in it. Brother Lawrence, who engaged in largely menial community tasks such as sweeping the kitchen and peeling potatoes, wrote, "Our sanctification doesn't depend upon changing our works, but in doing that for God's sake which we commonly do for our own... It's a great delusion to think that the times of prayer ought to differ from other times. We're strictly obliged to adhere to God by action in the time of action as by prayer in the season of prayer."

Following Christ was never meant to be comfortable, easy or safe, but rather impacting, tough and real
In addressing the topic of no holds barred discipleship, I've made various assumptions. They're as follows:

- We want to be challenged. So we approach the Father in sincerity and humility and pray with the Psalmist, "Search me, O God, and know my heart; test me and know my anxious thoughts. See if there is any offensive way in me, and lead me in the way everlasting" (Psalm 139:23–24).
- We recognize that we have a long way to go. If the apostle Paul admitted he wasn't the finished article, then so will we. In Philippians 3:12 he wrote, "Not that I have already obtained all this, or have already been made perfect..." We affirm with John Newton, "I'm not what I ought to be, I'm not what I'd like to be, I'm not what I hope to be, but I'm not what I was, and by the grace of God I am what I am."
- We're dissatisfied with how we are living our lives, but we're "confident of this, that he who began a good work in [us] will carry it on to completion until the day of Christ Jesus" (Philippians 1:6).
- God's Word is the absolute truth, and the truth hurts, but its hurting is for a purpose, which is "that the man [or woman] of God may be thoroughly equipped for every good work" (2 Timothy 3:17).

- We're prepared to be offended where the Word of God highlights areas in our lives which aren't submitted to Christ's lordship, because...

- We don't want to settle for consumer Christianity, a lowering of the bar, a false security, a twisting of the truth which offers all blessings at no cost, i.e. a shallow misrepresentation of the message of Jesus which many teachers promote because it satisfies what itching ears want to hear (2 Timothy 4:3). In our individualistic and self-centred societies, the following question is a particularly penetrating one: am I prepared to allow God to help himself to me, or am I simply consumed with what I want to make of my life?

When we take a close look at Jesus Christ, we see that he was a revolutionary, a radical, a shaker. If we listen to his voice, by definition what we hear will be revolutionary, radical, and shaking. During the pope's visit to Cuba in 1998, a slogan was daubed on a prominent wall: "To be a Christian without being a revolutionary is a mortal sin." To heed Jesus' call may be dangerous, costly, and unpopular. We will most likely at certain times be rejected, misunderstood, vilified, and slandered. So the reality is that if we truly decide to obey him, to translate our considered biblical literacy into biblical obedience, our lives will never be the same.

From the outset, we admit we're all weak, fickle, proud – basically, we've messed up and need God's help
We're inclined to put people on pedestals. We admire and aspire to emulate others, but there's a fine line between admiration and hero worship. Being on a pedestal is an isolated and lonely existence, which is surely why so many

"successful" Christian leaders drop out of the race – they end up actually believing the lavish comments people make about them or to them. The truth is we all have blind spots, weaknesses, and issues. So from the start, I want to acknowledge mine up front. I've messed up. I will continue to mess up. I've let myself, others, and God down, and will do so again in the future. I can't live up to my own standards, let alone God's.

As Proverbs 16:18 says, "Pride goes before destruction, a haughty spirit before a fall." I've always struggled with pride, which is such an ugly characteristic. It's so easy to criticize, find fault, judge, and condemn. I can easily see what's wrong with other people whilst failing to take the plank out of my own eye.

All of us yearn for acceptance, popularity, approval, endorsement. I'm no different. This means that even without wanting it to be the case, everything ends up being done with mixed motives. That's where key friendships are indispensable. For the last number of years I've been accountable to a team of friends from different backgrounds and walks of life, who have my permission to ask me probing questions, to challenge my motives, to highlight areas of compromise and inconsistency. It's been absolutely crucial – painful at times, to be sure, as I'm made aware of some of the ugliness and flaws of my personality – but it's helped me to refocus on seeking only the Master's approval.

Many of us feel condemned and discouraged at the apparent lack of impact we're having on our street, campus, office floor, on the team, or with our friends and family. Sometimes I'm amazed at my own fickleness – how there's a disconnect between what I profess and what I live out; or how I can sing God's praises in church but retreat demurely in the market place when his honour is at stake; or how I can appear so enthused about my faith with fellow believers yet so reluctant to share that same faith with non-believers, sometimes even when I'm handed a gift-wrapped opportunity.

I'm in good company with the apostle Paul though (and probably you are too), whose words provide such comfort as he wrestled with the same inconsistencies between wanting to please God yet so frequently falling short. He wrote, "I do not understand what I do. For what I want to do I do not do, but what I hate I do... What a wretched man I am! Who will rescue me from this body of death? *Thanks be to God – through Jesus Christ our Lord!*" (Romans 7:15, 24–25, italics mine)

Turning the world upside down again

Capon questions what has changed and where things went wrong:

What happened to radical Christianity, the un-nice brand of Christianity that turned the world upside down? What happened to the smashing, life-threatening, anti-institutional gospel that spread through the first century like wildfire and was considered (by those in power) *dangerous*? What happened to the kind of Christians whose hearts were on fire, who had no fear, who spoke the truth no matter what the consequence, who made the world uncomfortable, who were willing to follow Jesus wherever he went? What happened to the kind of Christians who were filled with passion and gratitude, and who every day were unable to get over the grace of God?

I want to play my part in turning the world upside down; I want to be fearless, bold, uncompromising and passionate in reaching out to the lost on behalf of the King of Kings; I never want to get over the grace of God; I want to be prepared to follow Jesus wherever he went; and I invite you to join me in this pursuit. As C. T. Studd declared, "If Jesus Christ is God and died for me, then no sacrifice can be too great for me to make for him." So may the God of grace help you and me to rediscover this dangerous, revolutionary, earth-transforming message, and translate it into our daily living.

CHAPTER THREE

Trust

You already know about how God lined everything up when I arrived in Burundi. But why did I go there in the first place? I'll rewind a bit further.

It was August 1998. I had been working as a business development executive – but for how much longer? "God, right now, if you want me to go to Burundi, then give me a sign. It's a hell-hole war zone, and it's going to mean leaving family, friends, money, security, everything. It'll involve radical changes in my life, so come on, right now, in front of the computer as I sit here, please give me a radical sign. I trust you." It was a specific prayer request, seeking a specific answer. Burundi had nothing to do with my job, and very few people knew anything about this isolated and largely forgotten country in the heart of the African continent. So I was asking God to do something extraordinary. If he answered clearly, I would go. It would mean letting go of everything I cherished and moving to a country with a different language, climate and culture, which was torn apart by an ongoing civil war.

I had recently finished living in the East End of London whilst attending Bible college. My regular prayer throughout that year had been, "God, I trust you. I'll do anything; I'll go anywhere. Just make it clear."

That's a prayer all of us can pray, no matter what stage of our lives we're at. It may be that we're in the right place for now, or maybe not. The bottom line for me was that it was a prayer of complete surrender. I cried out again and again to God, "Come on, Lord, you've got my whole life! Do whatever you want with it. I don't want security. I just want to be in your will; that's the safest place to be."

Slowly as the course came to an end, the other students were all getting their jobs – their "security" – lined up for the coming year. But security to me was a mixed blessing. If I had that kind of "security", then I wouldn't need to trust in God. I wanted to trust him alone for everything, knowing that in actual fact real and lasting security can only be found in him. So it was an exciting place to be, whilst at the same time a frustrating one, because I didn't sense any clear leading or guidance. It was now the last week of the course before we all went our separate ways, and I was as clueless as ever.

On the second last day, I was still waiting. "Lord, please! I'm 24, single, available, no strings, willing to go anywhere and do anything. I beg you, reveal your purposes for my life!" Someone gave me a piece of paper with a name and telephone number scribbled on it. A man had been trying to track me down. So I rang him, and we arranged to see each other the next day. It was now the end of my course. Was the answer about to come?

We met in central London, and after introducing himself, he said, "Simon, as I've been praying, the Lord has laid your name on my heart. How would you feel about working in Burundi?" As he said that, my heart started pumping faster. I had never seen or heard of this guy. Was this what the Lord had been making me wait for? He carried on talking, explaining how there were great needs among the youth in Burundi, and how the church was asking for trained personnel. Inwardly my mind was working overtime. I told him at the end of our meeting that I would "be spiritual and pray about it"(!), and then get back to him in due course.

The following Monday, I was back in the marketing department of my firm. I had prayed that audacious prayer of surrender and trust, and had asked for a sign about Burundi. I was fasting and expecting an answer. But how could the Lord possibly answer? Wasn't the demand for a sign about an obscure country in the heart of Africa a little unreasonable, all the more so as the marketing job had nothing to do with it? "God, come on, if you want me to go to Burundi, then give me a sign right now in front of the computer..." I waited, but not for long. I took a phone call, and the man on the other end of the line asked me a question out of the blue which took my breath away: "Do you know anyone who wants to work in Burundi?"

I was off...

How God calls is his call

Will God always speak that clearly? Must you have a similarly direct divine intervention? Was it really that easy? Well, not exactly. I had huffed and puffed on occasion with indignation and impatience, I had knocked on or tried to force my way through umpteen doors, I had "failed" or been rejected at interviews, I had fasted and prayed and moaned and groaned and sulked and stalled and sighed and sweated; but God had responded in his own good time, orchestrating the right job to come up at the right time for the right man.

There are no magic formulae or foolproof methods for

discerning God's call and direction for our lives. Sometimes
he dramatically writes it in blazing letters in the sky or uses
a phone call as was the case for me; other times he uses an
apparently insignificant throwaway comment or an obscure
lead through a newspaper. We can't be prescriptive in dic-
tating how God will guide and intervene. The important
thing is to trust him completely, even when the answer
seems painfully long in the coming, or when the heavens
reverberate in infuriating silence.

Two of the first verses I learned off by heart in my teens
at youth camp were Proverbs 3:5–6. It reads, "Trust in the
Lord with all your heart and lean not on your own understanding; in all your ways acknowledge him, and he will
make your paths straight." Easier said than done, you might
think. But there's no getting around the fact that God is calling us to radical trusting in every area of our lives. He promises to make our paths straight, although not necessarily
even or comfortable or tidy or attractive or welcoming. He
promises life to the full – a life of meaning, purpose, challenge, and impact – and he wants to be involved and
acknowledged in all our situations and decision-making,
both in the mundane and the exceptional. He calls us to
such a conscious realization of his presence that trust
becomes as natural an instinct to us as breathing. As
Chambers put it, "When you really see Jesus, I defy you to
doubt him. When he says, 'Let not your hearts be troubled,'
if you see him I defy you to trouble your mind, it's a moral
impossibility to doubt when he's there. Every time you get
into personal contact with Jesus, his words are real. 'My
peace I give you,' it's a peace all over from the crown of the
head to the sole of the feet, an irrepressible confidence.

'Your life is hid with Christ in God,' and the imperturbable peace of Jesus Christ is imparted to you."

Such trust results in inner peace and tranquility which defy personal circumstances and trials. Whatever life throws at us, we know Jesus is bigger. Even in death, he gives us total assurance and confidence to trust him and stand firm to the end.

Trust through life and death

The "peace of God which passes all understanding" releases us from the fear of death, and thereby enables us to maximize life. Hence the countless examples throughout history, including friends in Rwanda and Burundi, who when faced with death were absolutely calm and prepared. As Paul wrote triumphantly, "'Where, O death, is your victory? Where, O death, is your sting?'" (1 Corinthians 15:55) Jesus' death, according to Hebrews 2:15, was to "free those who all their lives were held in slavery by their fear of death".

When James Calvert took a team of missionaries with him and sailed to the Fiji Islands to attempt to minister to the cannibals there, the captain of the ship thought it was sheer lunacy. Imagine going to tell people about Jesus when all they want to do is eat you! The captain pleaded with Calvert to change his mind. "You fool! You will lose your life and the lives of those with you if you go among such savages." But Calvert was unstinting in his trust and resolve, and simply replied, "We died before we came here."

Personally I've come close to dying on a number of occasions in the last few years. People have also tried to dissuade me from undertaking risky journeys and missions.

Even committed believers have suggested we curtail our evangelistic activities upcountry. But all of us involved on these dangerous outings would testify that we've never felt closer to God than when driving along deserted roads which were the scenes of recent bloodshed. During one particularly tense period, my colleague looked across at me as I drove around a hairpin bend ripe for an ambush and exclaimed, "Simon, isn't it liberating? We are immortal until God calls us home!" We laughed in exhilaration. His words were so real. No rebel could touch us, unless the Sovereign Lord allowed it to happen; and if he allowed it to happen, then it meant he had decided our time was up, and he wanted us back home with him. We didn't have a death wish. We weren't complete idiots – but unlike others, we weren't ruled by fear. Our job was just to trust and obey.

The apostle Paul was familiar with danger. He wrote, "For to me, to live is Christ and to die is gain. If I am to go on living in the body, this will mean fruitful labour for me. Yet what shall I choose? I do not know! I am torn between the two: I desire to depart and be with Christ, which is better by far; but it is more necessary for you that I remain in the body" (Philippians 1:21–24). This resonates with me from my own experiences over the last few years. No matter how "nice" and comfortable we manage to make our lives, it's still a sick world in which we live. The injustice and suffering are overwhelming. So Paul's point is that however good this life is, he would rather have died and gone to heaven, where he would be free from the presence of sin in this world. But actually in the meantime he has plenty more work that God wants him to do. Knowing this to be the case, he gets on with it and maximizes his time, energy and resources in service of the King, up until the day that God calls him home, which he anticipates eagerly.

Our danger tends to be that we can't seem to trust God for our lives. We fear death and seek to avoid it at all costs. Home is here on earth, we think, and we want to stay here in as much comfort as possible for as long as possible. But such a mindset makes sense only for those with no conception of God; it's fundamentally inconsistent with the bigger picture the Bible paints for us.

Fear cripples many of us. It's the antithesis of trust, and prevents us from really living – not just fear of death, but also fear of the future, fear of financial insecurity, fear of failure, fear of rejection, fear of loneliness. But God's Word is very matter-of-fact in discussing the spiritual death which takes place in us when we surrender to Christ, and the resulting implications. Paul wrote, "Since, then, you have been raised with Christ, set your hearts on things above... Set your minds on things above, not on earthly things. For you died, and your life is now hidden with Christ in God. When Christ, who is your life, appears, then you also will appear with him in glory" (Colossians 3:1–4). So if we truly embrace this death to self, and this heavenly longing, then we will experience freedom from fear, because as David wrote, "Even though I walk through the valley of the shadow of death, I will fear no evil, for you are with me; your rod and your staff, they comfort me" (Psalm 23:4). We have the guaranteed hope and confidence that God is not only with us, but that when Christ appears, we "also will appear with him in glory"; and such promises are what will keep us trusting through the difficult times.

Trust through difficult times

When things go wrong, I quickly get discouraged. I wonder whether I could have done things differently, or whether I'm getting my just desserts. I sometimes even wonder whether the very bedrock of my life is a delusional faith which simply validates and explains some of my deeper experiences and questions. Trusting through difficult times isn't easy. Faced with problems, whether wholly innocent or complicit in how they came about, my knee-jerk reaction is often to feel hard done by, to shift the blame onto somebody else, to look for an easy way out. Turning to God and trusting him doesn't come naturally or instinctively – unless I recognize that trials are part and parcel of everyone's life.

If we recognize that God's aim with our lives is to make us more like Jesus, then we will submit to whatever discipline he deems appropriate. The writer to the Hebrews noted that "no discipline seems pleasant at the time, but painful. Later on, however, it produces a harvest of righteousness and peace for those who have been trained by it" (Hebrews 12:11). Peter wrote to those who "may have had to suffer grief in all kinds of trials". The purpose behind those trials was "so that your faith – of greater worth than gold, which perishes even though refined by fire – may be proved genuine and may result in praise, glory and honour when Jesus Christ is revealed" (1 Peter 1:6–7). God can be trusted, and isn't prepared to deal with us on our own terms. He lays down the conditions of our discipleship. He is the source of all knowledge and wisdom, and has our best interests at heart; and he will use anything or anybody to develop and transform us into what he wants us to be. Chambers writes,

God can never make me wine if I object to the fingers he uses to crush me. If only God would crush me with his fingers, and say "Now my son, I am going to make you broken bread and poured out wine in a particular way and everyone will know what I am doing." But when he uses someone who is not a Christian, or someone I particularly dislike, or some set of circumstances I said I would never submit to, and begins to make these crushers, I object.

I must never choose the scene of my martyrdom, nor must I choose the things God will use in order to make me broken bread and poured out wine. His own Son did not choose. God chose for his Son that he should have a devil in his company for three years. We say, "I want angels; I want people better than myself; I want everything to be significantly from God, otherwise I cannot live the life, or do the thing properly; I always want to be gilt-edged." Let God do as he likes. If you are ever going to be wine to drink, you must be crushed; grapes cannot be drunk; grapes are only wine when they are crushed. I wonder what kind of coarse finger and thumb God has been using to squeeze you, and you have been like a marble and escaped? You are not ripe yet, and if God had squeezed you, the wine that came out would have been remarkably bitter. Let God go on with his crushing, because it will work out his purpose in the end.

Yes, it will work out his purpose in the end. I choose to trust him for that. Sometimes through the tough times it's tricky to cling on, but God can be trusted, not just in our difficult times, but also more specifically in our doubts and uncertainties.

Trust through uncertainties

Life is full of uncertainties. Multiple variables are out of our control. We do our best to control as many facets of our lives as possible, but ultimately we can't predict everything that will happen around us and to us. However, in the life of faith, radical trusting won't fear those uncertainties, but will rather embrace them. Chambers notes, "The nature of the spiritual life is that we are certain in our uncertainties, consequently we don't make our nests anywhere... Certainty is the mark of the common-sense life; gracious uncertainty is the mark of the spiritual life. To be certain of God means that we are uncertain in all our ways, we don't know what a day will bring forth. This is generally said with a sigh of sadness; it should rather be an expression of breathless expectation. We are uncertain of the next step, but we are certain of God... Leave the whole thing to him, it is gloriously uncertain how he'll come in, but he will come."

So as we look towards the future, and lay down our own plans and agendas, we will remain unfazed by any unexpected twists and turns on our journey's path. After all, if we understood his ways, there would be no need for trust. And although we may be uncertain with regard to future plans, we do know that God's plans and purposes won't be thwarted (Job 42:2), so we can safely trust him and leave it to him to accomplish what he wants through us as his surrendered vessels. God can be trusted with our fears, our finances, our friends, our futures. We don't need to prepare our own "sensible" contingency arrangements, which are invariably just a respectable veneer acting as a mask for our lack of faith and trust in the character of God.

No worries!

The practical implications of total trust are astounding. Worrying loses its grip on our lives. Most of us are consumed with worry, but if we worry, we can't trust; conversely though, if we truly trust, we can't worry. As we grow in trust and dependence on the Lord, the more we experience the reality of his utter trustworthiness and dependability. At the risk of sounding too simplistic, it really is, in the words of the Lion King, "...no worries for the rest of your days, it's a problem-free philosophy, *hakuna matata*". Worry has been described as the interest we pay on tomorrow's troubles, and it severely curtails the extent to which we can act out our dreams and maximize our lives for Jesus.

A widow was telling her story to a reporter about how she had managed to raise a huge family which included six of her own and another twelve adopted children. Not only did they grow up into fine young men and women, but she had retained her own sanity and spirit through several tiring decades. Answering his question as to the secret of her success, she replied, "I managed so well because I'm in a partnership!" The reporter was confused by her answer, and asked, "I don't understand. Please explain what you mean." The woman replied, "Many years ago I said, 'Lord, I'll do the work and you do the worrying.' And I haven't had an anxious care since."

Worrying seldom helps. For each one of us, we can be certain that God's call will never take us where his grace won't keep us. Be it in the workplace or with family, we acknowledge the Lord's control and right to do with us as he wills. We trust his character and constancy. For parents, that brings real assurance for our children as we seek to raise them to be radically countercultural in standing up for Jesus. For Lizzie and me, taking our newborn son back to Africa where the quality of healthcare is decidedly ropey takes trust that God will watch over him. As Christians living out our faith in our jobs, neighbourhoods, at the aerobics class or the shops, we trust God to guide us, to use us, to empower and to equip us, so that we can take part in the privileged adventure of bringing hope, purpose, healing and restoration into people's lives in Jesus' name.

CHAPTER FOUR

Hanging in There

Two snapshots OF tropical tummy trouble:

1. It was probably malaria. Before dawn, after umpteen hot and cold sweats, and regular dashes to the lavatory, I got ready to go to the doctor. Not only was there no electricity, but the water had been temporarily cut off. I fumbled around barefoot in the dark, and didn't see a glass bottle left on the ground the night before. So I accidentally kicked it, and it shattered, spraying glass shards across the bathroom floor. In my feeble, dazed state, I prepared a stool sample (why is it called that?!); but to my horror discovered I hadn't taken the lid off the container, and faeces was everywhere, including all over my hands. So there in the dark I swayed, disorientated and feeble, barefoot amidst the broken glass, hands covered in mess, and no water to wash it off with!

2. I had been up all night, crawling to and from the bathroom where I had alternated positions with regard to the toilet, depending on whether it was the dysentery or the food poisoning that was winning the fight to exit from my exhausted body. Projectile vomit and diarrhoea meant that I was being emptied of everything within me, and it felt like I was shrivelling up until there would be nothing left. I stumbled back

to bed as the dawn light filtered through the curtains. I grabbed my Bible, asking the Lord in his mercy to give me a word of comfort. The pages opened to the book of James, and the first verses my eyes came upon were, "Consider it pure joy, my brothers, whenever you face trials of many kinds, because you know that the testing of your faith develops perseverance. Perseverance must finish its work so that you may be mature and complete, not lacking anything" (James 1:2–4).

I managed a wry chuckle, if not considering it pure joy! Mission work can be so very glamorous at times! Joking aside, there's no doubt that it's through our struggles and difficulties that we experience God's closeness to a greater degree. Joni Eareckson Tada, wheelchair-bound for many years since her diving accident as a teenager, wrote that "when life is rosy, we may slide by with knowing about Jesus, with imitating him and quoting him and speaking of him. But only in suffering will we *know* Jesus".

We all get tempted to give up, to throw in the towel, and to settle for less than God's best for us. Sometimes, if we're honest, knowing *about* Jesus is a more attractive option than knowing *him*, because the latter involves the pain of identifying with him in his death as well as in his life. I know my natural tendency is to take the easier option. But following Jesus was never meant to be a stroll in the park. He didn't promise us an easy life if we accepted his invitation. However, there's a purpose behind the hard times. Sanders wrote, "Trials are God's vote of confidence in us." Paul went so far as to say, "We also rejoice in our sufferings, because we know that suffering produces perseverance;

perseverance, character; and character, hope. And hope does not disappoint us, because God has poured out his love into our hearts by the Holy Spirit, whom he has given us" (Romans 5:3–5). As Madame Guyon said, "It is the fire of suffering that brings forth the gold of godliness."

So below we will take note of the perseverance of some of the greats of the past, before considering how we can persevere in the present, and prepare ourselves to persevere in the future.

Perseverance from the past

Today Christopher Columbus is a household name. Centuries after his exploits, people still remember and credit him with the discovery of the New World. However, it could easily have gone horribly wrong. His men on board were threatening mutiny because they had spent weeks without sighting land, and food supplies were dwindling. They were disgruntled and questioning his authority. The trip was nearly a disaster. He himself must have been tempted to turn back; but the last entry on his log at the end of each day simply read: "Today we moved *westward!*" He held on long enough and proved the words of Emerson that "there's no difference between heroes and ordinary people; the hero just fights five minutes longer".

The next "great" in our list is a man who made a disastrous first attempt in the world of business. He switched to politics but within only one year that didn't work out either. He tried his hand for a second time at business, but failed again. That meant three failures in three years.

He proposed to his fiancée after four years of courtship, but she turned him down. Another woman he was courting died some time later. All these pressures led to a nervous breakdown, which required two years of convalescence, after which he relaunched his aborted political career with a bid to be elected as speaker of the House of Representatives. He failed. He was again defeated two years later for the position of elector. Another three years after this, he was defeated as he ran for a seat in Congress. Another five years passed before he sought office again, but was defeated. Tragically his four-year-old son died during this time. That led to seven years in the wilderness, before running for the Senate – to no avail.

Things looked more positive the following year, when he was nominated by his party as their vice-presidential candidate, but his running mate and himself were defeated in the general election. He failed two years later when trying again for a seat in the Senate. However, another two years later, in 1860, after 24 years of dogged perseverance, Abraham Lincoln was elected as the 16th president of the United States of America!

Garibaldi, the great Italian patriot who led Italy many years ago to unification and freedom, said to those who would follow him, "I promise you forced marches, short rations, bloody battles, wounds, imprisonment and death, but let him who loves home and fatherland follow me."

This wasn't an attractive political manifesto – not what modern-day spin doctors would recommend to woo the electorate – but Garibaldi was a realist. He suffered greatly for his cause. Many of his men died. They needed to hold on through much trial and adversity. His aim required costly sacrifice and gritty tenacity. And he saw his costly dream come true.

William Carey is often attributed the title "father of modern missions". He was born into a desperately poor family, and consequently obtained a poor education. He was apprenticed as a shoemaker, but simply didn't make the grade. He tried his hand at running a school, but it functioned badly. His marriage was an unhappy one, during which his daughter died early – an event which left him bald for life. He was a deeply committed believer, but his subsequent attempt at pastoring a small church lessened his chances of ordination, because by common consent his sermons were too tedious and boring.

Despite such an apparently flawed track record, Carey formed a missionary society, with himself as the first candidate setting sail to India. This feeble individual translated the Bible into Bengali, Oriya, Marathi, Hindi, Assamese and Sanskrit, as well as portions into 29 other languages. At one stage, he lost ten years' translation work in a fire – what did he do? He just started again. Then there were contributions to literature, education, literacy, agriculture, getting infanticide outlawed and more. This man's obedience and perseverance were used to impact the lives of literally millions of people.

Before dying, knowing that one of his supporters wanted to write about his life, Carey conveyed his wishes: "If one should think it worth his while to write my life, I will give you a criterion by which you may judge of its correctness. If he gives me credit for being a plodder, he will describe me justly. Anything beyond this will be too much. *I can plod. I can persevere in any definite pursuit.* To this I owe everything."

For this man, the odds were stacked heavily against him. He had chosen to take on some of the most powerful traders, politicians and businessmen of his day, as well as most of the British royal family, and even the likes of Admiral Lord Nelson, who was a national hero. But there was no stopping him in his single-minded pursuit of justice for the victims of the slave trade. His dogged persevering through multiple setbacks, smear campaigns, ostracism and betrayal, lasted more than 50 years, but he had the joy of seeing his dream come to fruition shortly before he died, as Parliament formally abolished slavery. Constantly heckled and mocked, William Wilberforce was even beaten up a couple of times. One loyal friend of his sent him a light-hearted note saying, "I shall expect to read of you carbonated by West Indian planters, barbecued by African merchants and eaten by Guinea captains, but do not be daunted, for – I will write your epitaph!"

As the Second World War drew nearer, a young Japanese man called Sochira was trying to make a go of his business, manufacturing piston rings for Toyota. He had big dreams and was passionate about motorbikes, but had very limited capital to invest. Toyota's quality standards were too high for him, and after repeated attempts to develop adequate materials, he had used up all his funding. However, he risked everything in the pursuit of his dream by pawning his wife's jewellery.

Several months later, after many further setbacks and rejections, Toyota agreed to develop a partnership with him. A new problem arose by 1940 when he realized that he simply couldn't fulfil his orders any longer, because his factory was too small. The war effort meant that rationing had kicked in, so building materials were hard to come by if he were to construct a larger factory capable of meeting the new demands. His application for a cement permit was rejected, but he found a way of making his own cement.

Once his new factory was built, he expected things to run smoothly, but within a short space of time an American bombing raid left it in a heap of rubble. Undaunted, he simply knuckled down, rebuilt his factory, and resumed production. The same thing happened a second time as an air raid passed overhead and destroyed his livelihood. A third time he rebuilt, but an earthquake in 1945 wreaked renewed destruction. Surely he would give up!

But Sochira was a tenacious visionary. He was unwavering in believing his dreams would come to fruition. He rebuilt his factory for a fourth time, and quickly cornered the market by recycling military generator-engines and using them in the construction of his model of motorbikes. In 1952, after repeated experimentation and failure, but having persevered and developed his own engines, he launched his first "Cub" motorbike. Within ten years his surname was synonymous with motorbikes worldwide, and I myself own one of his models, a Honda 250cc.

If we are going to survive the contemporary crises in our own current circumstances, let's consider what we can learn from the likes of Columbus, Lincoln, Garibaldi, Carey, Wilberforce and Honda.

Perseverance in the present

We may be products of our past, but we certainly don't need to remain prisoners to it. Although he had been betrayed, assaulted and sold into slavery, Joseph was able to recognize a higher purpose behind those events as he reassured his brothers, "You intended to harm me, but God intended it for good to accomplish what is now being done" (Genesis 50:20). Despite his desperately grim illness, Hezekiah was able to declare, "Surely it was for my benefit that I suffered such anguish" (Isaiah 38:17). So we're not advocating that we embrace trials and sufferings with resigned acceptance, as if fate has dealt us a non-negotiable harsh hand of cards. However, we are saying that having wrestled and argued and made our case before the Lord Almighty, if circumstances don't pan out exactly as we would have desired, then we attempt to discern God's deeper purposes for us in any given situation.

Perseverance may be required in multiple scenarios – in the dull monotony of an unfulfilling career, in a financial quagmire which offers no end in sight, in a nasty situation at work which can't be resolved, in caring for a sick dependant who needs constant attention, in agonizing over a difficult child who shows no sign of progress, in maintaining dignified calm when an obvious injustice screams out for vengeful retribution.

Like it or not, the reality for all of us is that many aspects of living are mundane drudgery. Shopping, cooking, vacuuming, paying bills – none of these are exciting, dynamic, adrenaline-pumping activities. But they can't be ignored or avoided. As we've considered no holds barred discipleship, such humdrum chores didn't spring to mind. No, we immediately thought of glamorous, cutting-edge, dramatic, energizing, action-packed situations in which God used us to impact our society, our friends or our family. The truth is, he will use us in the latter, but more often than not, our call is outworked in regular consistent obedience and submission to his desire for our lives. Much of Wilberforce's work was correspondence, communication and lobbying. Lincoln's time was mostly used up with administration. Chambers notes, "It is inbred in us that we have to do exceptional things for God; but we have not. We have to be exceptional in the ordinary things, to be holy in mean streets, among mean people, and this isn't learned in five minutes."

Accepting the call to radical living may lead to rejection, vilification, slander. We may be objects of ridicule, scorn, even hate. At times we will be tempted to quit. C. T. Studd and his wife experienced intense rejection and hatred when they set up house in China. They slept on the floor in the most basic of conditions, and were perceived by the locals as white devils. He wrote of this period, "For five years we never went outside our doors without a volley of curses from our neighbours." Just try to imagine that! Even nowadays, some of us experience almost irrational hatred from our colleagues for our faith in Jesus Christ. But we need to be ready for such reactions, and persevere through such times. The aging apostle John warned the scattered believers, "Do not be surprised, my brothers, if the world hates you" (1 John 3:13). Jesus emphasized this to his disciples shortly before his crucifixion: "If the world hates you, keep in mind that it hated me first. If you belonged to the world, it would love you as its own. As it is, you do not belong to the world, but I have chosen you out of the world. This is why the world hates you" (John 15:18–19). Likewise some people hated the likes of Garibaldi, Columbus and Wilberforce. Paul's words to Timothy from the depth of his dank Roman dungeon are so matter-of-fact: "Everyone who wants to live a godly life in Christ Jesus will be persecuted" (2 Timothy 3:12).

When it comes to our spiritual lives, we can't be dependent on "highs" engendered through large meetings or conferences, because our lives are not lived out on a daily basis at such venues. We need to nurture our relationship with Christ through disciplined times of regular intimacy. Carey's ability to "plod" so effectively was earthed in an intimate personal relationship with Christ, with whom he spent many early morning hours in prayerful adoration. Like all of us though, he went through dry seasons during which it was a struggle to pray and prioritize time with the Lord. Perseverance is always required through such times of apparent distance and drought. C. S. Lewis talked of how sometimes people experience extraordinary times of intimacy and closeness to God. However, God "never allows this state of affairs to last long. Sooner or later he withdraws, if not in fact, at least from their conscious experience, all those supports and incentives. He leaves the creature to stand up on its own legs – to carry out from the will alone duties which have lost all relish. It is during such trough periods, much more than during the peak periods, that it is growing into the sort of creature he wants it to be."

Perseverance doesn't come naturally. All of those cited above must have longed to give up on numerous occasions and settle for less. In our own situations, thoughts and temptations often assail us about compromising, taking the easier option, or abandoning ship. Temptations manifest themselves with each of us in different ways – we may struggle with issues of self-worth, image, lust, food, exercise, money, laziness, greed, integrity. Unhealthy habits or cycles of behaviour may seem to have a hold on us, which induce crippling guilt. But Jesus knows what it is to wrestle with temptation. "For we do not have a high priest who is unable to sympathise with our weaknesses, but we have one who has been tempted in every way, just as we are – yet was without sin" (Hebrews 4:15). He knows the pain of temptation, because "he himself suffered when he was tempted, [and so] he is able to help those who are being tempted" (Hebrews 2:18).

So we never stop persevering and resisting, despite sometimes feeling helpless and overpowered by temptation's onslaughts. There's always hope, because as Paul says, "No temptation has seized you except what is common to man. And God is faithful; he will not let you be tempted beyond what you can bear. But when you are tempted, he will also provide a way out so that you can stand up under it" (1 Corinthians 10:13). Jesus came through his time of temptation in the wilderness with power for ministry, and temptation can similarly be used by God to strengthen us and empower us for greater exploits for his glory. As Chambers notes, "God permits temptation for it does to us what the storms do to the oaks – it roots us; and what the fire does for the paintings on the porcelain – it makes them permanent."

When a friendship or a business partnership seems to be breaking down, we need to hang on in there. To pull through will require both endurance and tenacity. Chambers highlights the difference between the two as follows: "Tenacity is more than endurance, it is endurance combined with the absolute certainty that what we are looking for is going to transpire. Tenacity is more than hanging on, which may be but the weakness of being too afraid to fall. Tenacity is the supreme effort of a man refusing to believe that his hero is going to be conquered."

We who have responded to the call to no holds barred discipleship have faith that our Hero will never be conquered! The Bible describes faith as "being sure of what we hope for and certain of what we do not see" (Hebrews 11:1). And we too "are more than conquerors through him who loved us" (Romans 8:37). We're on the winning side. So despite the issues in our lives and the temptations to give up or compromise, we choose to "resist the devil, and he will flee (James 4:7). We may take knocks along the way, but we refuse to label events as failures, or to be discouraged by these apparent setbacks. We insist that there is a huge difference between failing and becoming a failure. The only way we become a failure is by pulling out of the race and giving up. But as we struggle on being holy in mean streets, in mean situations, with mean people, we will grow stronger, we will see progress, and we will bring glory to the King.

Perseverance for the future

My first spiritual mentor left his dying wife and four children for a young man. The teacher I idolized most at Bible College left his wife and daughter for a younger woman. Both of these men had been much used by God in many different settings in a number of countries – but they didn't persevere, and they didn't finish well. We want to learn how to persevere for the future so that we do finish strong. It's futile to start well if we don't finish the race.

John Akwiri was a Tanzanian marathon runner at the Mexico Olympics. Marathons are never easy, but the blistering heat compounded the difficulties for those involved. However, the race was duly completed in a reasonable time, and other events reclaimed the focus for the crowds gathered in the stadium. Several hours later, as the day's activities had just come to an end, people were emptying out of the stands and heading home. Just then Akwiri entered through the tunnel and embarked on his last lap. His face was contorted in agony, his cramped feet shuffled along, and progress was painfully slow. Gradually the crowd caught on and started cheering wildly. When Akwiri crossed the finishing line, the noise was deafening. At a later press conference, he was asked by the interviewer, "You were so far behind. Why didn't you just give up?" He replied, "My country didn't send me here to start the race, but to finish it." I don't know the name of a single gold medal winner at the Mexico Olympics – they were before my time. But I do know the name of an obscure African who came last in the marathon. His name was John Akwiri. He finished his race.

In seeking to finish the race, and finish well, we will need persistence and determination. We will press on through trials and difficulties. Finishing strong is not a matter of talent or genius – examples of unsuccessful men with talent and unfulfilled women with genius are everywhere to be seen. It's not a matter of education or social standing, but of disciplined, dogged, tenacious persevering, walking closely in Jesus' footsteps, heeding his call, obeying his commands, fulfilling his commission.

I want to persevere; I want to finish well. I guess you do too. Wang Mingdao, who spent over 20 years in prison as part of the persecuted underground church in China, made the observation, "You Christians in the West – many of you start well, but few of you finish well." How can we make sure we do finish strong? Observing the common characteristics of those who have already done so is probably the best place to start.

Two leading researchers into the area of leadership, Stanley and Clinton, made detailed studies of followers of Jesus and drew conclusions from reams of data as to what were the commonalities of those who did indeed last the course and finish the race without dropping out or faltering towards the end. They listed the following key characteristics, which provide a good check list for you to see how you are faring:

1. They had perspective which enabled them to focus.
2. They enjoyed intimacy with Christ and experienced repeated times of inner renewal.
3. They were disciplined in important areas of life.
4. They maintained a positive learning attitude all their lives.
5. They had a network of meaningful relationships and several important mentors during their lifetime.

So in referring to these points, ask yourself some searching questions – not to feel condemned, but to highlight areas where you might slip up:

1. Perspective involves seeing the bigger picture and having structured long-term goals to work with and aim at effectively. Do you have perspective which enables you to focus?

2. Repeated times of intimacy and renewal are the basis of any lasting relationship. Are you committed to nurturing this most important relationship of your life?

3. Without discipline in whatever area you are dealing with, the result is underperformance and unrealized potential. Are there key areas of indiscipline in your life which need to be addressed?

4. One of Stanley and Clinton's tragic observations is that most people stop learning by the age of 40 and from that time onwards live on what they have previously learned, rather than continuing to grow in depth of spirituality and knowledge. How about you? Are you still hungry to grow more and more in love for Jesus, for the Bible, and for people?

5. Close intentional friendships involving vulnerable accountability and openness enable people to challenge, encourage, affirm and rebuke each other in a safe and loving context. Do you have such relationships in place?

One of the most enriching experiences and network of relationships I have had since leaving the UK has been an intentional group of seven men to whom I send my spiritual journal once a week through email, and they are free to pick up on anything that strikes them. It has proved highly beneficial, as I seek to persevere and remain radically sharp and effective to the end. "As iron sharpens iron, so one man sharpens another" (Proverbs 27:17).

If you're not involved in such a group (or it could just as well be with one other person), I would encourage you to see how instrumental it might be in your journey of faith. If you want help and a structure to such a relationship, Foster lists five questions to ask each time you meet:

1. What experiences of prayer and meditation have you had this week?
2. What temptations did you face this week?
3. What movements of the Holy Spirit did you experience this week?
4. What opportunities to serve others have you had this week?
5. In what ways have you encountered Christ in your study of the Bible this week?

As the aging and suffering apostle Paul came to the end of his life in a dank dungeon, he was able to write triumphantly to Timothy, his younger partner in the gospel, "I have fought the good fight, I have finished the race, I have kept the faith. Now there is in store for me the crown of righteousness, which the Lord, the righteous Judge, will award to me on that day – and not only to me, but also to all who have longed for his appearing" (2 Timothy 4:7–8). Well, God help us, like Paul, to persevere to the end!

I remember watching the 400 metres at the 1996 Atlanta Olympic Games. Derek Redmond was representing Great Britain. This was the culmination of months and even years of gruelling training and preparation, with his dad as trainer and coach. He was out in front, when his Achilles tendon snapped, and he pulled up in agony. He stopped running but didn't drop out of the race. He hobbled forward, lifting his injured leg step by step. As happened with Akwiri, the spectators rose to their feet and cheered him onwards. The pain was so excruciating that they wondered if he would be able to finish the race. But then a grey-haired man jumped over the railings and ran towards him. He put his arms around Derek's waist and together they made it to the finishing line. That other man was his father. During post-race interviewing, Redmond told the press, "He was the only one who could have helped me, because he was the only one who knew what I'd been through." Jesus similarly comes alongside each of us to carry us the rest of the way. With his help, we will finish the race. And he is the only one who can do it, because he is the only one who knows what we've been through, and what lies ahead.

I'll close with an extract from an email I wrote in September 2001:

Supergranny Guillebaud graduated to glory in Rwanda on the 12th September, aged 86! On her last day in action, she preached energetically for an hour in her widows' meeting, which had been planned and prepared for a long time. For some reason she said goodbye to them (as if she knew she was homeward bound!). The last photo of her taken alive was of her gingerly dancing with the widows before the Lord. She then went home for a game of scrabble, had a stroke in the night, and died peacefully two days later. What a woman of God! What a challenge! To me, her complete surrender in every aspect of her life was an absolutely logical out-working of the realization that heaven is our home, not here. So come on, where's the next generation? Here I am, send me! I want to be part of it. Count me in! Let's seek his face and not settle until we know the answer to the question: where do I/you fit into his plan? Or is he relegated to fitting into my/your plan...? Let's run until we drop!

CHAPTER FIVE

Time on Our Knees

We're too busy to pray, and so we're too busy to have power. We have a great deal of activity but we accomplish little; many services but few conversions; much machinery but few results.   R. A. Torrey

An isolated rancher had requested the district superintendent to assign his community a pastor.

"How big a man do you want?" enquired the superintendent.

"Well, brother," the rancher replied, "we're not overly particular, but when he's on his knees we'd like to have him reach heaven."

Libraries are packed full of books on prayer, so in a sense there's nothing to be added. Most Christians agree that prayer is of paramount importance in our lives, that its purpose is to provide us with power for our daily living – yet there's frequently a disconnect between what we profess and what we make time for. So as we address the call to radical living, let's briefly take a look at the primacy of prayer, the purpose of prayer, and the power of prayer.

The primacy of prayer

We know many familiar scriptures exhorting us to prayer. Colossians 4:2 says, "Devote yourselves to prayer." 1 Thessalonians 5:17 calls on the believers to "pray continually". Ephesians 6:18 tells us to "pray in the Spirit on all occasions with all kinds of prayers and requests". It's a serious business. Most of us are too busy to pray, but our excuses illustrate our fundamental misunderstanding of the primacy of prayer. If we grasp the importance of prayer, it will undergird our very existence and act as the engine-room for all our activities, such that we will be too busy not to pray, as the title of a book on the subject suggests. 2 Chronicles 7:14 says, "If my people, who are called by my name, will humble themselves and pray and seek my face and turn from their wicked ways, then I will hear from heaven and will forgive their sins and heal their land." The conditions laid down by the Lord seem clear. Are we willing to listen to him?

I live with many people who don't know where the money for this month's rent will come from, or how the children will be able to go to school for lack of available funds, or even whether they'll have enough food to eat today. My friend Janine sees the Lord reply miraculously on a constant basis as she seeks to provide for a household that has grown to include 56 orphans. She said to me a while back, "Simon, when there's no food on the breakfast table, I don't worry. I've done my bit by being obedient to God in taking them in. Now the Lord must be faithful!" She repeats what George Mueller, that great man of prayer, used to frequently express in different ways. On one occasion, his orphans' home in Bristol had run out of money. He had never asked anyone for money, and they had never lacked for food; but on this particular morning there was literally nothing in store as the children sat at the breakfast table waiting to eat. Mueller calmly said, "Children, we're about to witness a miracle." Successive knocks at the door saw the baker arrive with extra bread which he had felt "prompted" to get up earlier to bake for them, and the milkman, who had just experienced problems outside their house on his round, and so was offering all his milk to them before it went off! Our Father is faithful. We're just so slow to believe...and to trust...and to pray.

We frequently hear about revival. Some are living in constant expectancy that it's around the corner. Others are disillusioned, having been promised it for so long by their leaders and yet not having experienced it. Out in Burundi, friends experienced the glorious outpouring of revival a few decades ago. Our AIDS project manager, Nathan, was converted at the time, and he was filled with such passion that he walked hundreds of miles around the country with other zealots, praying constantly and proclaiming the gospel as he went. For them back then, as for us in our day, the common denominator as passionate believers is that we desperately long for and pray for revival (although when it comes it is always messy and offensive to large sections of the Body of Christ, as it was out here in the East African revival). But, as Tozer insists, "Prayer for revival will prevail when radical amendments to lifestyle are made, not before." Are we willing to make those costly radical amendments to our lifestyles?

James O. Fraser was a remarkable man who became largely forgotten as he laboured for many years in isolation behind the great mountain ranges of China's far west. His work was amongst the unreached Lisu tribespeople. In areas steeped in witchcraft, he fasted and prayed for years with hardly any tangible spiritual fruit. Through dark times he contemplated suicide, but clung on to God's promises, until the day came when he knew he had reached the place of victory. The battle in prayer had been won. In God's time there was a massive outpouring of the Holy Spirit in revival power, and in village after village where previously the inhabitants had been hardened to the gospel, families responded en masse. Fraser reflected on his work and concluded the following: "I used to think that prayer should have the first place and teaching the second. I now feel that prayer should have the first, second and third place, and teaching the fourth."

Spending time before the Lord in praise and adoration, in confession and intercession, in petition and anticipation, is of paramount importance. Jesus placed prayer right at the heart of his ministry. He modelled the life of prayer, and exhorted his disciples to follow his example. As a matter of fact, he never taught his disciples to preach, but he made sure they were well taught in the school of prayer. We need to access power from God before we can wield power with men. Hence speaking with God will come before speaking with men. It's said that Francis of Assisi spent 75 percent of his active hours in prayer and 25 percent in preaching and apostolic service; yet although he's primarily remembered nowadays for the impact of his preaching, the latter was only the result of many hours spent in the Father's presence, before being sent out empowered, envisioned, energized and equipped by the Holy Spirit.

For many, prayer isn't the first choice, but a last resort. However, hopefully if you've carried on reading this far, you're determined not to make it a last resort; but maybe you're hesitant – can I really trust God? What if... Well, if that's you, just cry out to God with Whitefield, "Lord, help me to begin to begin." Jo Church, who was one of those most intimately involved in the East African revival, prayed, "Lord, send revival, beginning in me." Another of Whitefield's great prayers was, "Oh that I might work for eternity; pray for eternity; preach for eternity: I want only God." Yes, Lord, I want that radical hunger for more of you!

The purpose of prayer

The purpose of prayer is not to coerce God into getting involved in our world so as to solve our problems, but to help us to enter into his world, gain his perspective, and fulfil his purposes. As O. Hallesby said, "Prayer has one function and that is to answer 'yes' when Christ knocks." Spurgeon once said that "prayer pulls the rope down below and the great bell rings above in the ears of God. Some scarcely stir the bell, for they pray so languidly; others give only an occasional jerk at the rope. But he who communicates with heaven is the man who grasps the rope boldly and pulls continuously with all his might".

If we want to be fruitful in our lives and deeply impact society, it will mean time on our knees. I was recently challenged by a Bolivian Christian called Carlos. He had decided to follow Jesus at significant cost, experiencing alienation and antagonism from various family members. But slowly through the years all his family had softened and likewise decided to surrender their lives to God. What was his secret? "Three times a day, year after year, I got down on my knees and pleaded with the Lord for all my family." I'm now doing the same for my own family.

God has ordained prayer as the means to access his power, and there's no other way to see his Kingdom Reign break through in our lives. At the turn of the 20th century, two pastors' wives were sitting mending their husbands' trousers. One of them said to the other, "My poor Andrew, he's totally discouraged in his work at church. He told me yesterday he was thinking of packing it all in. Nothing seems to go right for him."

The other replied, "Well, for my husband it's the complete opposite. He's so vibrant and on fire, it seems like the Lord is closer to him than ever before."

There was a subdued stillness as they continued to mend their husbands' trousers – the first one patching the seat and the other the knees.

Paul frequently used the metaphor of war to convey the urgency and purpose of prayer. We're in a battle, and "the weapons we fight with are not the weapons of the world. On the contrary, they have divine power to demolish strongholds" (2 Corinthians 10:4). The realm of warfare we're engaging in isn't the material world, rather the spiritual one (Ephesians 6:10–18), which is why he exhorts us to "put on the full armour of God, so that when the day of evil comes, you may be able to stand your ground, and after you have done everything, to stand" (verse 13). In turn he calls us to appropriate every available weapon in God's spiritual armoury (verses 14–18). The list of weapons culminates with prayer: "And pray in the Spirit on all occasions with all kinds of prayers and requests. With this in mind, be alert and always keep on praying for all the saints. Pray also for me..." (verses 18–19).

So we need an active awareness and acknowledgement in our daily existence that all of us have a key contribution to make in God's army, and that prayer plays a crucial role. Otherwise, our prayers will be sluggish, apathetic, weakened and blunted. Piper highlights the critical issue as follows: "Probably the number one reason why prayer malfunctions in the hands of believers is that we try to turn a wartime walkie-talkie into a domestic intercom. *Until you know that life is war, you cannot know what prayer is for...* But what have millions of Christians done? We have stopped believing that we are in a war. No urgency, no watching, no vigilance. No strategic planning. Just easy peace and prosperity. And what did we do with the walkie-talkie? We tried to rig it up as an intercom in our houses – not to call in fire power for conflict with a mortal enemy, but to ask for more comforts in the den."

Urgent, persevering, impassioned, broken-spirited, desperate intercessory pleading will lead (under God's sovereign hand) to revival, which we all long to see. God is sovereign and cannot be manipulated. Yet he chooses to honour the prayers of his people when they answer his call to bow down humbly before him, seek his face, and acknowledge and turn from their sin. Evangelist R.A. Torrey wrote his own prescription for revival in any church, community or city, based on his analysis of past revivals:

First: Let a group of Christians get thoroughly right with God. If this isn't done, the rest will come to nothing.

Second: Let them bind themselves together to pray for revival until God opens the windows of heaven and comes down.

Third: Let them put themselves at the disposal of God

for his use as he sees fit in winning others to Christ. That is all. I've given this prescription around the world... and in no instance has it failed.

It cannot fail.

If we were to commit ourselves to such a course of action, not even the sky would be the limit as God would honour his promises to bestow his power on us to accomplish his purposes and change his world. But what of this power? Is it really available to me? If so, how can I appropriate it?

The power of prayer

Pengwern Jones was a close friend of John "Praying" Hyde. What he observed of Hyde is worth including at length because it can teach us so much:

> I owe him more than I owe to any man, for showing me what a prayer-life is, and what a real consecrated life is. I shall ever praise God for bringing me into contact with him... The first time I met him was at Ludhiana in the Punjab, where he lived at the time. I had been invited to speak a few words on the Revival in the Khassia Hills to the Conference of the United States Presbyterian Mission, who had their annual session at the time there. I had traveled by night from Allahabad to Ludhiana, and reached there early in the morning. I was taken to have a cup of tea with the delegates and others, and I was introduced across the table to Mr. Hyde. All that he said to me was, "I want to see you; I shall wait for you at the door." There he was waiting, and his first word was,

"Come with me to the prayer room, we want you there."
I do not know whether it was a command or a request. I
felt I had to go. I told him that I had traveled all night,
and that I was tired, and had to speak at four o'clock, but
I went with him; we found half a dozen persons there,
and Hyde went down on his face before the Lord. I knelt
down, and a strange feeling crept over me. Several
prayed, and then Hyde began, and I remember very little
more. I knew that I was in the presence of God himself,
and had no desire to leave the place; in fact, I do not
think that I thought of myself or of my surroundings, for
I had entered a new world, and I wanted to remain there.

We had entered the room about eight o'clock in the
morning; several had gone out, others had come in, but
Hyde was on his face on the floor, and had led us in
prayer several times. Meals had been forgotten, and my
tired feeling had gone, and the revival account and message that I was to deliver – and concerning which I had
been very anxious – had gone out of my mind, until
about three thirty, when Hyde got up, and he said to me,
"You are to speak at four o'clock; I shall take you to have
a cup of tea." I replied that he must need a little refresh-
ment, too, but he said, "No, I do not want any, but you
must have some." We called in at my room and washed
hurriedly, and then we both had a cup of tea, and it was
full time for the service. He took me right unto the door,
then took my hand and said, "Go in and speak, that is
your work. I shall go back to the prayer room to pray for
you, that is my work. When the service is over, come into
the prayer room again, and we shall praise God
together." What a thrill, like an electric shock, passed
through me as we parted. It was easy to speak, though I

was speaking through an interpreter. What I said, I do not know. Before the meeting was over, the Indian translator, overcome by his feelings, and overpowered by the Spirit of God, failed to go on, and another had to take his place. I know the Lord spoke that night. He spoke to me, and spoke to many. I realized then the power of prayer; how often I had read of blessing in answer to prayer, but it was brought home to me that evening with such force that ever since I try to enlist prayer warriors to pray for me whenever I stand up to deliver his messages. It was one of the most wonderful services I ever attended, and I know that it was the praying saint behind the scenes that brought the blessing down on me.

I went back after the service to him, to praise the Lord. There was no question asked by him about whether it was a good service or not, whether men had received a blessing or not; nor did I think of telling him what blessing I had personally received and how his prayers had been answered. He seemed to know it all, and how he praised the Lord and how easy it was for me to praise the Lord, and speak to Him of the blessing He had given.

I recently devoured the book containing the above passage, as I hungered for the effectiveness in intercessory prayer of the likes of John Hyde. I was back by myself in Burundi, separated from my precious Lizzie and unborn son for what would be several months. I had arrived back heavy-hearted, my malaise compounded by my mother's freshly diagnosed cancer. However, what followed were days of unparalleled intimacy with Jesus. Largely undisturbed early from the crack of dawn and late into the evenings, I could spend hours in God's presence, seeking his face, praising him, and engaging in intercessory prayer. I share an entry from my journal of that season to illustrate some lessons learnt from spending real concentrated time in the Lord's presence:

29th September: I'm reading this book on Praying Hyde, and it's so challenging. As I tried to emulate him by letting rip in prayer for ages on my bed in the dark, it suddenly struck me that these few months will probably be my quietest ones for the next several decades! So instead of bemoaning my loneliness, this could be the most fabulous time of nurturing intimacy with the Lord by spending as much time with him as possible. Let's be positive! I'm rubbish in general with my own company, but loved the chance tonight to pray so undisturbed – not something I really did much over the last few months of hectic preaching around England. So, Lord, I give you this time, I surrender my life afresh, have your way, do whatever you want with me. What a great privilege it is to be a child of the King!

30th September: It's my fasting day. I feel caught up in an extraordinary state at the moment, somewhat a mountain-top experience. It surely has to do with the fact that I'm spending so much time in the Lord's presence – what a numbskull I am and how slow to learn the fact that intimacy, which we all crave, can only be attained and sustained through disciplined commitment and time given to him. *We want effortless intimacy, but it just doesn't happen that way.*

So I was up at the crack of dawn, and jumped out of bed with a "Good morning, Jesus!" I prayed passionately, sang, read the Bible and then started preparing a sermon for Sunday. I wanted to make notes on the computer, but it seemed like it had fused with the latest power cut. The power wouldn't go on, although everything else electrical was working. I prayed over the computer, and went off to start searching the Scriptures for the right message. I came back to find it working! And then the sermon just flowed as never before. The Lord was being so clear, the ideas and structure flowed so easily. Truly preparation of the messenger is as important as preparation of the message.

God knows how long this season of beautiful intimacy will last, but in any case I want to maximize it. Keep the discipline, Simon, and guard the time spent in his presence. Don't let business crowd him out. It's so obvious, and we all know prayer is of paramount importance, but Satan will do anything to distract us from what renders him powerless. I remember someone once asking me, "How much do you want of God?" Because "nobody has less of God than they want". Keep me hungry and thirsty for more of you, dear Lord!

1st October: ...Whilst I was in the bath in the evening, Bruno came round, and so I knew he'd be back again shortly. Instead of viewing him as a nuisance who wanted to use up my valuable time to improve his English, I decided to see him as someone sent by God to come to faith through me. But before reading this Praying Hyde book I would've just prayed: "Right, Lord, Bruno's coming round. Please open the eyes of his heart to see you, and give me the right words. May he come to know you." Such a piddly prayer would take about twenty seconds. Instead I really prayed, and spent serious time, delaying supper until I'd done so. I worshipped away on the guitar, and proclaimed the Lord's victory until my fingers were too sore to carry on. I was full of faith, so claimed his life for Jesus, and interceded on his behalf.

Then Bruno showed up again. He's a nice lad, 22 years old, we chatted about football, studies, etc., and then I asked him what he thought about Jesus – was he ready to face judgement? Basically I then led him through the gospel and asked him if he wanted to receive Christ as his Lord and Saviour right now – no pressure – but do you want to be ready? He did! I prayed and he repeated after me. He's coming with me to church on Sunday. Seal your work in his life, O Lord!"

Throughout the ages there have been powerful and compelling manifestations of the power of prayer in individuals' lives. In 1540, Luther's close friend and assistant, Frederick Myconius, grew more and more ill until he knew his death was imminent. Sensing his impending departure, he scribbled a farewell scrawl to Luther, who read the note and hurriedly dispatched his reply: "I command you in the name of God to live because I still have need of you in the work of reforming the church. The Lord will never let me hear that you are dead, but will permit you to survive me. For this I am praying, this is my will, and may my will be done, because I seek only to glorify the name of God." Myconius could no longer even speak when Luther's reply arrived, but in due course he did recover, enjoying six further fruitful years until his death, a couple of months after Luther!

Dr Helen Roseveare was a missionary in Zaire across the

lake from me. She tells of a young mother dying at the mission station shortly after having given birth prematurely. The medical staff needed a makeshift incubator for the premature baby, but the only hot water bottle they had leaked. During team prayers that morning, the children were asked to pray for the baby and her little sister who was now orphaned. So one young girl prayed, "Dear God, please send a hot water bottle today. Tomorrow will be too late because by then the baby will be dead. And, dear Lord, send a doll for the sister so she won't feel so lonely." Although parcel deliveries were rare, a large one did arrive that afternoon. They opened it and were overjoyed to find a hot water bottle! The little girl who had prayed so earnestly pounced on the parcel and rummaged amongst the contents, exclaiming, "If God sent that, I'm sure he also sent a doll." She was right! A beautiful doll was there, in response to the little girl's petition. The Sovereign Lord had ensured five months previously that a group of ladies should pack just the right contents to arrive to the nearest day at an obscure mission station thousands of miles away!

The first weekend I arrived in Burundi, I was invited upcountry with the Scripture Union team. It was a disastrous trip with four breakdowns, so we missed most of the meetings. I returned angry and discouraged that many people had missed out on hearing the gospel simply because we didn't have a vehicle which worked properly. SU was in debt, but had so much potential to be used for God's glory. So I sent out an email asking for prayer for two things: i) to get SU out of debt, and ii) to buy a truck for evangelism around the country. In response to that email, I envisaged $25,000 coming in over the following month. What happened? A cheque for $8,000 arrived, given specifically for a vehicle, and over the coming month $25,000 came in. God answers prayer.

I'm involved in a streetkids project called New Generation, which is run by an inspiring friend called Dieudonné. He enjoys reminiscing about the day they were all going hungry as a group. As they prayed, they asked the Lord to provide not just someone's scraps for them; rather in faith they asked for the Lord to provide them with an amazing meal. At that very moment elsewhere in the capital, I was leaving an embassy function, and there was tray after tray of delicacies, all of which were to be thrown away. So I asked if I could take them for the street children, and a few minutes later arrived at New Generation's office to hand over the ambassador for the USA's food to these cute little hungry, faith-filled ambassadors for Christ!

God is interested in every aspect of our lives, both the seemingly trivial and the undeniably important. Nothing is too small for him, whether it's a water bottle, a doll, and a sandwich, or a car, a career, or calling. He wants us to ask, he's waiting to hear, and he's longing to reply. Andrew Murray said of prayer, "God's giving is inseparably connected with our asking. Only by intercession can that power be brought from heaven which will enable the Church to conquer the world." George Mueller, who fed several thousand orphans simply in answer to prayer, said that he never came to requests or petitions in prayer until he had "an active and living realisation of the presence of God". Hudson Taylor, after so many painful breakthroughs in China, wrote, "The prayer power has never been tried to its full capacity. If we want to see mighty works of Divine power and grace wrought in the place of weakness, failure and disappointment, let us answer God's standing challenge, 'Call to me, and I will answer you, and show you great and mighty things, which you do not know.'"

Maybe I should decide to call out more loudly, boldly and persistently, so that God will show me "great and mighty things" of which I do not know. Maybe I'll pray bigger prayers, as I'm naturally inclined to pray little ones. Maybe I'll pray more risky prayers, as I'm all too good at offering up qualified petitions couched in religious verbiage to lessen my disappointment if my will isn't done. Maybe I'll pray more specific prayers, as I'm an expert at vague ones which are hard to see whether they've been answered or not. Maybe I'll pray more uncomfortable and dangerous prayers, in case I've set the bar at a safe height and am missing out on more lofty exploits for God's glory. And for each one of us, maybe we can appropriate this anonymous prayer for ourselves: "Disturb me, Lord, when my dreams come true, only because I dreamed too small. Disturb me when I arrive safely, only because I sailed too close to the shore. Disturb me when the things I've gained cause me to lose my thirst for more of you. Disturb me when I've acquired success, only to lose my desire for excellence. Disturb me when I give up too soon and settle too far short of the goals you have set for my life."

A word of encouragement...

Having spoken of the power of prayer, I want to recognize that there are plenty of uncertainties, irreconcilables, and mysteries in our lives and in our spiritual walks with the Lord Jesus. Some of us Christians insist on having all the answers, offering trite solutions to immeasurably complex issues. But it's just not that straightforward, is it? We can be plagued with doubts and fears. Am I in the right place? Or did I discern wrongly what I believed God was saying? Amidst such apparently impenetrable clouds, we may simply have to cling on to him, and cry out with Thomas Merton, "My Lord God, I have no idea where I am going. I do not see the road ahead of me. I cannot know for certain where it will end. Nor do I really know myself, and the fact that I think I am following your will does not mean that I am actually doing so. But I believe that the desire to please you does in fact please you."

There's a certain type of bamboo in Asia which grows to prodigious heights and at prodigious speeds – sometimes as much as 60 feet in six weeks. However, before that growth spurt, the seed lies in the dark beneath the ground for up to five years. Those farmers who make a profitable living from the bamboo would have given up long ago and changed crops if they didn't know that plenty was going on beneath the surface despite the fact that there was no visible sign to encourage their perseverance. Every bit of watering and waiting is worthwhile. No prayer is wasted.

All too often I feel a miserable failure in the area of praying. So Brother Lawrence brings me much relief when he says that "for many years I was bothered by the thought that I was a failure at prayer. Then one day I realised that I would always be a failure at prayer; and I've got along much better ever since". Merton's line above also brings me great comfort. My desire to please God does in fact please him. Yes, God, thank you that my desire to please you pleases you! And in a sense, we'll always be beginners dipping our toes below the surface of the unplumbed depths of prayerful intimacy with God Almighty. So whilst not resigning ourselves to a mediocre prayer life or a staid, lifeless routine in prayer, we'll get along much better, as Brother Lawrence said, by acknowledging our own limitations and casting ourselves on the mercy of God. Along similar lines, Merton also said, "We do not want to be beginners. But let us be convinced of the fact that we will never be anything else but beginners all our life!"

A commitment prayer

Let's end both this chapter and Part One with a solemn prayer of commitment to God which Tozer penned last century. The consequences of such praying, when heartfelt, are quite simply earth-shaking. Families, communities, regions and nations have been and still can be changed by people who have surrendered their right to themselves and have been willing to give their all for the glory of Jesus Christ. Maybe read it over several times, check that you're willing to pray it wholeheartedly, and take time to grapple with the implications that each line will have for your relationships, career, family and future…

Here goes:

I come to you today, O Lord,
To give up my rights,
To lay down my life,
To offer my future,
To give my devotion, my skills, my energies.
I shall not waste time
Deploring my weaknesses
Nor my unfittedness for the work.

I acknowledge your choice with my life
To make your Christ attractive and intelligible
To those around me.
I come to you for spiritual preparation.
Put your hand upon me,
Anoint me with the oil of the One with Good News.
Save me from compromise,
Heal my soul from small ambitions,
Deliver me from the itch to always be right,
Save me from wasting time.
I accept hard work, I ask for no easy place,
Help me not to judge others who walk a smoother path.
Show me those things that diminish spiritual power in
   a soul.
I now consecrate my days to you.
Make your will more precious than anybody or anything,
Fill me with your power
And when at the end of life's journey I see you face to
   face
May I hear those undeserving words,
"Well done, you good and faithful servant".
I ask this not for myself
But for the glory of the name of your Son.

Part Two:

No Holds Barred Discipleship –
Why live radically?

CHAPTER SIX

Choose Life!

This day I call heaven and earth as witnesses against you that I have set before you life and death, blessings and curses. Now choose life.   Deuteronomy 30:19

The glory of God is a person fully alive.
                    Irenaeus, second century theologian

I'd rather be ashes than dust! I'd rather that my spark should burn out in a brilliant blaze than it should be stifled by dry rot. I'd rather be a superb meteor, every atom of me in magnificent glow, than a sleepy and permanent planet. The proper function of man is to live, not to exist. I won't waste my days in trying to prolong them. I'll use my time.   Jack London

In the cult film *Trainspotting*, the opening clip shows heroin-addict Renton fleeing from his pursuers. Above the hypnotic and pulsating background music, his deadpan voiceover lists several dozen choices. In the 1990s, those words attained iconic status and were printed on a poster which adorned many a student's wall. His speech culminates as follows:

Choose leisure wear and matching luggage. Choose a three piece suite on hire purchase in a range of ****ing fabrics. Choose DIY and wondering who you are on a

Sunday morning. Choose sitting on that couch watching mind-numbing spirit-crushing game-shows, stuffing ****ing junk food into your mouth. Choose rotting away at the end of it all, pissing yourself in a miserable home, nothing more than an embarrassment to the selfish, ****ed-up brats you've spawned to replace yourself. Choose your future. Choose life.

It's a raw and cynical list reflecting the grim pessimism which his circumstances embody; and although his desperate life – centred around finding the next fix – isn't representative of most people's lives in our contemporary society, the sentiments he expressed clearly resonated at a deep level with many. Life is largely meaningless. Why not at least experience the escape and euphoria of an amazing drug trip? He challenges us to offer a better alternative. What choice do we have?

Meet Larry Walters

Well, the following very ordinary man made his own remarkable choice. Few will have heard of Larry Walters. He was a 33-year-old truck driver living in San Pedro, not far from Los Angeles. On weekends he used to just sit around and watch TV. But this particular Saturday, he was bored with his usual routine, so he decided he wanted to *do* something. He went shopping and bought 42 weather balloons and a deck chair. Returning home, he anchored the chair to the ground with some ropes, and then tied the weather balloons to it. When all was ready, he ensconced himself in the chair, with his air gun nestled in his lap. He then cut the ropes, and rose steadily into the sky.

Within minutes he had attained an altitude of 16,000 feet. The air traffic control tower at LA airport reported receiving a number of garbled and incredulous messages from different pilots along the lines of, "You're not going to believe this, but there's a man floating up here in a deck chair!" Soon Larry's thirst for action seemed quenched, and he decided it was time to return to planet earth. He shot a number of balloons with his air gun and gradually floated downwards. Forty-five minutes later he landed at Long Beach, about seven miles from where he had taken off.

His excursion made front page news, resulting in a Timex ad and an interview on *The Tonight Show*. Quizzed as to his motivation for doing it, Larry Walters replied, "It was something I had to do – I couldn't just sit there!" He was able to quit his job and embark on a lucrative speaking tour as a motivational guru!

There are so many people in the world who "just sit there". This is nothing new. In the 19th century, Thoreau wrote, "The mass of men lead lives of quiet desperation." Whether at work or play, most people resign themselves to less than purpose-filled living. We've already noted that we'll all die – but how many of us will really live? As an ancient sage warned, "Fear not that your life shall come to an end, but rather that it shall never have a beginning."

So many people aspire to being "successful", yet find that when/if attained, success simply doesn't deliver the desired sense of wholeness. The brilliant but tragic Ernest Hemingway wrote shortly before committing suicide, "I live in a vacuum that's as lonely as a radio when the batteries are dead." Bob Geldof's autobiography is entitled *Is that it?*

According to Samuel Butler, "Life is one long process of getting tired." Actor Kenneth Williams wrote in his diary on the day of his death, "What's the bloody point?" Shakespeare wrote of life, "It is a tale told by an idiot, full of sound and fury, signifying nothing." Longfellow said that life was "but an empty dream", Thomas Browne that it was "but the shadow of death", and O. Henry that it was "made up of sobs, sniffles and smiles – sniffles predominating". Twentieth century philosopher Albert Camus said, "What is intolerable is to see one's life drained of meaning. To be told that there's no reason for existing. A man can't live without some reason for living." Jean-Paul Sartre noted, "This world isn't the product of intelligence. It meets our gaze as would a crumpled piece of paper...what is man but a little puddle of water whose freedom is death?" A. E. Matthews joked sadly of his own life, "In the end I got so old and tired and weary of living, that I looked in *The Times'* obituary column each morning and if I wasn't there, I got up!"

Taken together, they're enough to make anyone depressed! Contrast the words of Professor Joad, who was converted from atheism to Christianity. He said that "trying to find happiness from this world is like trying to light up a dark room by lighting a succession of matches. You strike one, it flickers for a moment, and then it goes out. But when you find Jesus Christ, it's as though the whole room's suddenly flooded with light."

More than a job

The problem in dismissing God from their lives is that those who do so must find an adequate alternative or substitute.

For some, careers become their whole raison d'être and consume their lives. But this rarely works. We may have a job, but do we have a life? For many, jobs are simply viewed as a means of paying the bills, and having enough disposable income to indulge in whatever form of entertainment enables one best to escape the dreary monotony of the workplace. As one of the staff sardonically quipped in the hit comedy *The Office*, "Put the key of despair into the lock of apathy. Turn the knob of mediocrity slowly and open the gates of despondency – welcome to a day in the average office."

Some have the privilege of a fulfilling job, though unfortunately many do not. Either way, life is about more than just work, and we all have multiple roles – as colleagues, parents, sons, daughters, spouses, neighbours, team-mates or friends. Those who still seek to acquire their sense of worth, value or acceptance wholly through their job titles are invariably left disappointed. But for the follower of Christ, a job is infused with added significance, such that even the mundane can be sacred if done for the glory of God. A job becomes more than just a job. It becomes a means of expressing our worship and gratitude to our Creator God.

Three men were working on a large building project, when a journalist from the local newspaper came and interviewed them. They were each asked, "What are you doing?" "I'm mixing mortar," grunted the main bricklayer. The second man said, "I'm helping put up this great stone wall." When the third man was asked, he replied, "I'm building a cathedral to the glory of God." All were engaged in the same process, but they each had a different attitude and perspective on what they were doing. Similarly for each one of us, whether we're administrators or teachers or artists or managers or whatever else the Lord has called us to, Paul encourages us to "work at it with all your heart, as working for the Lord, not for men" (Colossians 3:23).

The higher aim of bringing glory to our Creator is what will set followers of Jesus apart. We're marching to the tune of a different song sheet, and it sounds a radically different sequence of notes.

No regrets

Part of my own personal mission statement declares that "I'll endeavour to seize every appropriate opportunity for learning and growth so that I end up with no subsequent regrets". Choosing life means seizing the day, seizing the hour, seizing the moment. Robin Williams sought to inculcate this attitude in his pupils in the film *Dead Poets' Society*: "*Carpe diem!* Seize the day!" As the cliché goes, destiny isn't a matter of chance, it's a matter of choice. We only have one life on this earth, and Paul exhorts us to be making "the most of every opportunity, because the days are evil" (Ephesians 5:16).

A family friend writes about a documentary on five young Australian lads who had just done an 1,800-mile cycle ride through Outer Mongolia. They were interviewed about their time – how they had handled injuries, conflicts, and other unforeseen difficulties. The interviewer then asked, "Why did you do the trip?" The last boy said that when he was younger, he had a dream, and in the dream, he stood at the end of his life before five judges who were there to pass judgement on his life. After a long silence, one of the judges threw down the gavel and said, "Guilty of a wasted life!" He said that the dream had impacted him greatly, and he didn't want to get to the end of his life and hear the verdict pronounced, "Guilty of a wasted life!"

The friend concludes, "This young man wasn't a Christian. Are the children of the world more switched on than the children of light? Do we forget that one day we'll all stand before a Judge, not just in a dream, but in reality, and we'll be required to give account of all the deeds we've done and how we've used our talents?"

Back in 1996, I was part of a team that drove a truck for a mission organization from Wales to Kenya. We travelled through thirteen countries and had many eventful experiences over several months. Having returned to the UK, one of the women on our team wrote to me with the following reflections, "To me the calling I left Africa with wasn't just a call to evangelism, it was surpassing that call – it was a call to *live* for Jesus. Whatever country I'm in, I know God calls me to *live* for him. Not for a car, a job, family, church, Bible study, security, romance, friendships, or anything else I might want to live my life for. That's how God has started to change me since our trip. It used to be important what I ate, how much sleep I had – such trivial things I'd revolve my life around."

My longing – both for myself and for each one of us – is that when we get to the end of our lives, we won't be harking back to missed opportunities. We won't be fearful of the impending pronouncement, "Guilty of a wasted life!" We won't ruefully surmise that we've revolved our lives around trivialities. Rather we'll be able to look back with satisfaction at opportunities seized, gifts maximized, risks taken, obstacles overcome, storms weathered, people impacted, and our calling fulfilled. It will take our all to heed God's call. As Guinness writes, "Calling is the truth that God calls us to himself so decisively that everything we are, everything we do, everything we have is invested with a special devotion and dynamism lived out as a response to his summons and service."

What I'm not suggesting is a constant, pressurized, restless striving devoid of enjoyment and leisure. "Every good and perfect gift is from above, coming down from the Father of the heavenly lights" (James 1:17) who lavishes love on his children (1 John 3:1). He's a Father who loves us extravagantly, and who certainly doesn't want us to live under a crushing burden of inadequacy or self-imposed unattainable standards. Some of us indulge in an imbalanced self-punishing and introspection. Choosing life involves fully embracing and enjoying God's awesome creation and the opportunities which life presents us with. An anonymous friar, looking back on his life during his latter years, declared, "If I had my life to live over again, I'd try to make more mistakes next time. I'd relax, I'd limber up, I'd be sillier than I've been this trip. I'd take more trips. I'd be crazier. I'd climb more mountains, swim more rivers, and watch more sunsets. I'd eat more ice cream and less beans! If I had to do it over again I'd go places, do things, and travel lighter. If I had my life to live over I'd start barefooted earlier in the spring and stay that way later in the fall. I'd ride on more merry-go-rounds. I'd pick more daisies."

I remember a few years ago arriving home on my motorbike to find a concerned house guard. He handed me a letter and told me that some people were wanting to know my whereabouts. The letter contained various unfounded accusations, and made clear that if I didn't meet their demands, they would kill me. One chilling line said that they were going to cut out my eyes. It was an unpleasant incident, and I was forced to sleep over at a friend's house in another part of town for a while, and vary my routes wherever I drove. I returned on one occasion to find them waiting for me with a grenade, but was waved away by an onlooker before I got too close.

Although I had a few nightmares, I look back on that time and deeply value the insights and lessons it taught me. The prospect of death – or what seemed almost worse to me, losing my eyes – highlighted afresh what an incredible gift life is – and, more particularly in this case, sight. I had always taken my eyes for granted. Sight had been a right. But now I realized what a precious gift it was, as was my coordinated body capable of enjoying sport, as was the ability to read and write, to enjoy good food, to appreciate the beauty of the mountains, to touch and feel, to smell and sing, to be creative. The very threat of having my sight taken from me accentuated the richness of all such experiences. Since that time, my life has been lived with a deeper sense of gratitude and a heightened sensual awareness and appreciation; and so I consider those traumatic events as a defining epiphany in my life. From that moment, I wanted to *live* every day all the more. Each moment, however mundane, became infused with a new vibrancy and meaning.

Such was Russian author Fyodor Dostoevsky's experience when the czar had him arrested as a dissident and rebel, and sentenced him to death. The czar enjoyed toying with his prisoners by having them blindfolded and lined up in front of a firing squad. But only blanks were used, so the blindfolded prisoners heard the shots but weren't killed. They were invariably traumatized (one lost his mind on the spot), having undergone the process of dying yet avoiding death. The effect on Dostoevsky was life-transforming. His senses were sharpened such that every mouthful became more tasty, the songs of the birds more beautiful, the myriad shades of the leaves more delectable, the textures of fabrics more subtle; it was this very experience which enabled him to see things more deeply and convey them more richly in his writings.

The richness of life

I remember feeling chastened on one occasion when I had recently come out to Africa. I was feeling lonely and homesick, and a man called Livingstone came to visit me. As I wallowed in self-pity, he gently reminded me of his own situation. He had fled civil war in his homeland but then got caught up in the Congolese troubles, so had walked for 30 days through hundreds of miles of jungle. He had a bullet wound in his back to show for it, and hadn't seen or heard of his wife and children for six years. As a refugee he had minimal rights, no job, a hovel to sleep in, and a seemingly bleak future. Yet despite his personal circumstances, Livingstone was truly alive, counting his blessings, full of the Holy Spirit; and *he* had come around to encourage *me*, even though I had so much more than him. I realized that he was one of many African men and women who through the crucible of suffering had been elevated to loftier heights of intimacy with their heavenly Father.

Livingstone's attitude taught me (and can teach each one of us) that we can choose to be grateful for what we've been given rather than to complain about what we don't have.

And in choosing either the former or the latter response, it will become a habit for life. So may God help us to choose to be grateful people, because grateful people are joyful people, whose joy can defy personal circumstances. Paul said, "I have learned the secret of being content in any and every situation, whether well fed or hungry, whether living in plenty or in want. I can do everything through him who gives me strength" (Philippians 4:12–13).

Often as I pray I run through the many blessings in my life, be they material or spiritual: a roof over my head, the ability to read and write, availability of clean water, a full stomach, a functioning body, access to health services, precious family and friendships, freedom of speech and religion, a personal relationship with the Almighty God, assurance of forgiveness of sins, freedom from guilt, a guaranteed eternal inheritance, and the list goes on. We've so much to be grateful for, and therefore to live for.

Although no doubt our personal circumstances and trials are less extreme than Livingstone's, there are nevertheless so many uncertainties in life that it's natural for our human nature to seek to minimize them by controlling as much as possible. We like to have our ducks lined up, and our natural inclination is to play safe. However, it's those very uncertainties which define life as an adventure to be lived, and scream out to us to live lives of faith rather than tightly reined risk-minimization enterprises. Jesus enacted his very own promise of coming "that they may have life, and have it to the full" (John 10:10). He didn't promise longevity of life, but fullness of life. He himself only had a relatively short life, but it was a full one. Similarly I don't desire a long life per se, but a full one. Many octogenarians die before beginning to live. Abraham Lincoln was right when he wrote, "And in the end, it's not the years in your life that count. It's the life in your years."

So Keith Johnson suggests two alternatives: "There are those who like to say 'yes', and there are those who prefer to say 'no'. Those who say 'yes' are rewarded by the adventures they have; those who say 'no' are rewarded by the safety they attain." As followers of Jesus, we have the choice to embrace or reject a life of meaning, purpose, fulfilment, and challenge. Are we going to settle for the safety of existing, or will we choose to embark resolutely on the adventure of living? Jesus is calling each one of us. Will you say yes, or will you say no? Choose life! You won't regret it.

Chapter Seven

Death and Glory

The rebels had attacked the capital. I was preaching in the United States when I received the news. Emails trickled through: "Your offices have been taken over by the rebels as a launching pad for their attack on the military installation..." "No news as to which of your colleagues may have been killed..." "The army has retaliated, and many lie dead..." It was a horrible time of uncertainty. Eventually I discovered that none of my colleagues were among the 300 dead, although our neighbour was. But it shocked me further to discover that most of the dead were forcefully conscripted eleven- to fifteen-year-old child soldiers, sent into battle as cannon fodder by their cowardly superiors.

Throughout history child soldiers have been used in many conflicts. They've rarely chosen such a way of life. Rather they've usually been kidnapped and beaten into submission. One child soldier was a twelve-year-old bugler called Willie. He was an orphan and far from home, but he had a vibrant Christian faith, and despite constant abuse and opposition he sought to share the love of Christ with the older men in his regiment. It was a struggle, exacerbated by the fact that he slept in the tent containing the most ruthless and vulgar men – they vilified, mocked, slandered and scorned his every attempt to get alongside them. These were battle-weary and hardened men with blood on their hands.

One night, some of the military equipment was damaged

irreparably, and the commander was livid. The crime was a serious one and consequently so would be the punishment. An example would be made of the perpetrator. All evidence pointed to the one infamous tent where the worst and most insubordinate soldiers slept. A court martial was held, during which the commander called out to those assembled, "Now we know this squad contains whoever's guilty. So if the responsible party will step out like a man, the rest will go free."

Nobody moved. The commander became progressively more irate. "Come on! One of you is guilty. Step out now and receive ten lashes, and I give you my word that whoever comes forward will enable all the others to go free."

Still nobody moved. The commander was furious by this time, and barked angrily, "Don't mess me around! Whoever did this, come forward, otherwise you'll all get the ten lashes."

After what seemed an eternity of deafening silence and stillness, Willie shuffled forward and stammered, "Sir, you gave your word that whoever came forward and accepted to be punished would receive the ten lashes, and then all the others will be set free."

The commander was momentarily flabbergasted, but once the initial surprise had subsided he hollered at the other assembled men, "You bunch of cowards! We all know that Willie's not responsible for this crime. Come on! Ten lashes will finish him off. Whoever did it, be a man and come forward to receive your just desserts."

"With respect, sir," stammered Willie, "you gave your word, and you cannot go back on it now."

So Willie was stripped and tied up in front of all the men, who were so ashamed that their heads were bowed low and their eyes were glued to the floor. As the whip flailed repeatedly against his skin, Willie began to whimper until the guilty man, Jim, couldn't bear it any longer. He leapt forward and begged the commander to desist. "Stop! Stop! Sir, I should be tied up and flogged. That boy's innocent, I'm the guilty man. Set him free and tie me up, I'm the one who should be punished."

But through clenched teeth and searing pain, Willie whispered, "No, Jim. The commander gave his word. I've taken the punishment. You're free." He eventually passed out and was carried away to the camp hospital to be attended to. The following morning, the commander stopped at the door of Willie's hospital room and peered through the crack to observe Jim, the hardest and most cruel man in the regiment, on his knees next to the boy's bed. "Oh, Willie, why did you do it?"

Willie smiled weakly, and whispered, "Ah, Jim, I wanted you to know this: I did it so that you might know that this is what Christ did for you; only he did so much more. I suffered for one sin, but he suffered for all our sins. He loves you, Jim."

Willie died shortly afterwards, but as a result of that remarkable encounter of grace, so did the old Jim. The new Jim became a totally transformed man through Willie's enactment of the gospel, and he surrendered his old nature to the One who had died for him.

Jim's no different from many men I've come across in the bleak prisons of Burundi who have committed heinous crimes but have been touched by the power of grace. They've been forgiven much, and consequently they love much. They've grasped the fact that they must die a costly death to themselves, their past, and their twisted actions, because Jesus calls us to emulate his radical example and follow in his footsteps.

Dietrich Bonhoeffer wrote, "When Christ calls a man, he bids him come and die." Why should we care what this long-deceased German had to say about following Jesus? What weight is there behind his words? Why should we listen to him? Because just like Willie, Bonhoeffer was willing to pay the ultimate price for following Jesus. During the Second World War, he left the safety of exile in America and returned to suffer with his people and fight for liberation from the yoke of the Nazis, who eventually caught and executed him shortly before the end of the war. When people demonstrate and act out their willingness to die for what they believe, their words tend to carry more weight. His choosing life meant literally embracing death. For most of us it won't involve physical martyrdom. But Bonhoeffer himself knew – and calls us in turn – to embrace the challenge that if you haven't found something worth dying for, you haven't found something worth living for.

In John Chrysostom's final sermon, which led to his exile and death in 407 AD, he thundered, "The waters are raging and the winds are blowing but I have no fear for I stand firmly upon the rock. What am I to fear? Is it death? Life to me means Christ, and death is gain. Is it exile? The earth and everything it holds belongs to the Lord. Is it loss of property? I brought nothing into this world and I will bring nothing out of it. I have only contempt for the world and its ways and I scorn its honours."

His confidence in Christ is awe-inspiring on the one hand, and yet utterly logical on the other – but just because something is logical doesn't imply it's straightforward. It might be very difficult, because the cost may be great, as indeed it is if we heed Christ's call. However, as we deliberately choose to die to ourselves, we surrender or forfeit the right to ourselves, and thus the Holy Spirit has free rein to accomplish his sovereign purposes in and through our lives. The apostle Paul expands on this in his epistle to the Romans (6:3–8, 11–12, emphasis mine):

> Or don't you know that all of us who were baptised into Christ Jesus were baptised into his *death*? We were therefore buried with him through baptism into *death* in order that, just as Christ was raised from the *dead* through the glory of the Father, we too may live a new life. If we have been united with him like this in his *death*, we will certainly also be united with him in his resurrection. For we know that our old self was crucified with him so that the body of sin might be done away with, that we should no longer be slaves to sin – because anyone who has *died* has been freed from sin. Now if we *died* with Christ, we believe that we will also live with him… In the same way, count yourselves *dead* to sin but alive to God in Christ Jesus. Therefore do not let sin reign in your mortal body so that you obey its evil desires.

A few chapters later, Paul goes on, "For if you live according to the sinful nature, you will *die*; but if by the Spirit you put to *death* the misdeeds of the body, you will live, because those who are led by the Spirit of God are sons of God" (Romans 8:13–14). Christ's death on the cross was to set us free from the shackles of sin and open up a better way of life. As Peter writes, "He himself bore our sins in his body on the tree, so that we might *die* to sins and live for righteousness" (1 Peter 2:24). The dying to self is the pathway to life, as Paul wrote to Timothy, "If we *died* with him, we will also live with him" (2 Timothy 2:11). So Christ's death has huge consequences on our outlook and motivation for life. "For Christ's love compels us, because we are convinced that one *died* for all, and therefore all *died*. And he *died* for all, that those who live should no longer live for themselves but for him who *died* for them and was raised again" (2 Corinthians 5:14–15).

Many of our spiritual forebears speak of a time when they experienced this spiritual death. George Mueller was known by people around the world for the extraordinary answers to his prayers on a continual basis. One day he was urged to share the secret of the effectiveness of his ministry and prayer life. In his answer he spoke of his "secret death". "There was a day," he said, "when I died; utterly died." He spoke deliberately and quietly, bending lower until he nearly touched the floor. "I died to George Mueller, his opinions, preferences, tastes and will; died to the world, its approval or censure; died to the approval or blame even of my brethren and friends; and since then I have studied only to show myself approved of God."

Dying to one's own opinions, preferences, tastes and will, dying to the approval or censure of the world, and dying to the approval and blame of friends and family are supremely challenging. I know for myself I desperately long for acceptance, endorsement, popularity, significance. I want to receive the praises of other people. I want affirmation and recognition. I thirst for success. Yet the drive for success can be a positive or negative impulse, depending on the root motivation. And what's perceived as being successful varies according to whose standard you use. In Western society, we're pigeon-holed in an instant by our answer to the questions, "Who are you and what do you do?" Based on the answer, people like to ascertain how "impressive" and "successful" we are, and put us in a box. But the question is not "who" but "whose" you are; and in marked contrast to most people's yardstick of success, Chambers describes it as follows: "We are not called to be successful in accordance with ordinary standards, but in accordance with a corn of wheat falling into the ground and dying, becoming in that way what it never could be if it were to abide alone."

As history shows, a grain of wheat falling into the ground and dying has huge potential repercussions. Tertullian, in his great apology for the Christian faith, challenged the Roman authorities, "Kill us, torture us, condemn us, grind us to dust. The more you mow us down, the more we grow, for the seed of the church is the blood of the martyrs." It may shock us to learn that there were more martyrs last century than in all the previous centuries added together. Our brothers and sisters around the world are being put to death on a daily basis under regimes which are ideologically or religiously hostile to Christianity. Yet in places like China, in the face of persecution, prejudice, imprisonment, torture and death, the church of Jesus Christ has experienced times of explosive growth.

Death – be it a spiritual dying to self or even a literal laying down of one's life – sounds like such a dire and even macabre concept; and it would be if not for the events of that first Easter Sunday. No holds barred discipleship means living with the glorious hope of the resurrection, the certainty of ultimate victory, the assurance of sins forgiven, and the anticipation of eternal life. Yes, death will be swallowed up in victory! Ultimately, as someone once wrote, "Death isn't extinguishing the light from the Christian; it's putting out the lamp because the dawn has come." Is that really true?

Future Glory

An aging Harry Rimmer wrote the following letter to his friend Dr Charles Fuller:

I believe you're going to speak about heaven next Sunday. I'm interested in that land because I've held a clear title to a bit of property there for about fifty years. I didn't buy it, it was given to me without price, but the Donor purchased it for me at a tremendous sacrifice. I'm not holding it for speculation, it's not a vacant lot.

For over half a century I've been sending materials up to the greatest Architect in the universe, who's been building a home for me, which will never need re-modelling, because it'll suit me perfectly and will never grow old. Termites can never undermine its foundations, for it rests on the Rock of Ages; fire can't destroy it, floods can't wash it away; no bolts will ever be placed upon the doors, for no vicious person will ever enter the land where my dwelling stands.

It's almost completed and almost ready for me to enter in and abide in peace eternally without fear of being ejected. There's a valley of deep shadow between this place where I live and that to which I shall journey in a short time. I can't reach my home in that City without passing through this valley. But I'm not afraid because the best friend I ever had went through that same valley long long ago, and drove away all its gloom. He's stuck with me through thick and thin since we first became acquainted fifty-five years ago. And I own his promise in printed form, never to forsake me or leave me alone. He will be with me as I walk through the valley of the shadow. And I'll not lose my way when he's with me.

My ticket to Heaven has no date marked for the journey; no return coupon; no permit for baggage. I'm ready to go and I may not be here when you're talking next Sunday evening but I'll meet you there some day.

Harry Rimmer died before the following Sunday.

Verses abound throughout the Bible about our eternal hope in Christ. Peter writes, "Praise be to the God and Father of our Lord Jesus Christ! In his great mercy he has given us new birth into a *living hope* through the resurrection of Jesus Christ from the dead" (1 Peter 1:3, my emphasis). Our hope is a living one. The opposite of hope is despair, and it brings death. I was driving along one of the main roads in Burundi's capital one day and a hunched old woman dressed in rags walked out and began crossing. She didn't even look up. Her face was weary and haggard. I hooted the horn, slammed on the brakes and swerved, but she barely looked up. She was the epitome of despair, and a walking corpse. It broke my heart. Although she was still alive, she had died inside. She provides an extreme illustration of many people we interact with on a daily basis. Multitudes of lives are shrouded and swamped in suffocating despair. Yet there is hope.

The writer to the Hebrews says that "faith is being sure of what we *hope* for and certain of what we do not see" (Hebrews 11:1). Shortly before Moody graduated to glory, he said, "Someday you'll read in the papers that D. L. Moody is dead. Don't you believe it! At that moment I'll be more alive than I am now; I'll have gone up higher, that's all! I was born of the flesh in 1837; I was born of the Spirit in 1856. That which is born of the flesh may die, but that which is born of the Spirit will live forever!"

Biblical hope is a confident expectation which we can depend upon. This is in sharp contrast to today's usage in common parlance, which almost assumes uncertainty. People "hope" that things will work out, but there's often little confidence that it will. For such people who are "separate from Christ", they are "foreigners to the covenants... *without hope* and without God in the world" (Ephesians 2:12). Concerning their future after death, they "grieve like the rest of men, who have *no hope*" (1 Thessalonians 4:13); whereas the Christian can echo the confidence expressed by Paul to Titus, "We wait for the *blessed hope* – the glorious appearing of our great God and Saviour, Jesus Christ" (Titus 2:13).

In my own life in Burundi, it's this hope which keeps me keeping on. Things can appear so bleak, unfair, desperate and hopeless. A recurring prayer over the years at our daily team times of devotion, particularly during periods of more intense fighting, has been, "*Imana yacu, turagushimiye kuko watuzigamye kugez' uyu musi*" (Our Lord, we praise you that you have protected us until today). Yet it's the hope of heaven which sustains my brothers and sisters through the horrors of war. They're ready to die. That's why they risk their lives on the roads travelling upcountry, to take this message of hope to those dying in darkness and despair. We have a "faith and love that spring from the *hope* that is stored up for [us] in heaven and that [we] have already heard about in the word of truth, the gospel" (Colossians

1:5). So "we rejoice in the *hope* of the glory of God" (Romans 5:2). "And *hope* does not disappoint us, because God has poured out his love into our hearts by the Holy Spirit, whom he has given us" (Romans 5:5).

A fellow missionary out here saw an old man in grubby clothes at one of the many displacement camps. She wondered what his story was, and so approached him to find out. This man was in his eighties. He had seen his wife and children hacked to death and his house burnt down. He had walked many days to get to the camp, and had lost just about everything he ever owned, except the rags on his back. Yet at the end of his story of horrific personal loss, he was able to declare, "I never realized Jesus was all I needed until Jesus was all I had." What hope! Owning nothing, yet realizing that with Jesus he had everything he needed. Heaven was his home, and he's there now, enjoying eternal life with his loving heavenly Father. He was stripped of everything and physically destitute, but knew where he was going, and so could echo Paul's words, "But our citizenship is in heaven. And we eagerly await a Saviour from there, the Lord Jesus Christ, who, by the power that enables him to bring everything under his control, will transform our lowly bodies so that they will be like his glorious body" (Philippians 3:20–21).

Back in the 19th century, Mr Dickson was attempting to dissuade John Paton from going to the South Sea Islands as a missionary. He said, "You'll be eaten by the cannibals!" But Paton replied, "Mr Dickson, you're advanced in years now, and your own prospect is soon to be laid in the grave, there to be eaten by worms; I confess to you, that if I can but live and die serving and honouring the Lord Jesus, it'll make no difference to me whether I'm eaten by cannibals or worms; and in the Great Day my resurrection body will arise as fair as yours in the likeness of our risen Redeemer!"

No matter how hard our current circumstances are, "we have this *hope* as an anchor for the soul, firm and secure" (Hebrews 6:19). Buffeted by life's storms, this hope brings the "peace of God which transcends all understanding" (Philippians 4:7), as well as deep unshakeable joy. Paul prayed for the Romans, "May the God of *hope* fill you with all joy and peace as you trust in him, so that you will overflow with *hope* by the power of the Holy Spirit" (Romans 15:13). The only stipulation is that we "continue in [our] faith, established and firm, not moved from the *hope* held out in the gospel" (Colossians 1:23). When my friend Sara heard that her husband had been murdered in an ambush, she returned to her four children at home. No husband, no money, no job. How could the kids carry on at school? She was all alone. But she said to me, "Simon, you know, God is truly wonderful. I lost everything, and went home into my bedroom and cried out before the Lord. And he was there. He is amazing, and meets all my needs. My husband is now free of all this mess, and I share that same certain hope." Her face shone as she spoke.

Jesus himself must have been tempted to avoid his appointment with the cross, because he was "tempted in every way, just as we are – yet was without sin" (Hebrews 4:15). We read of his agonizing pleas in Gethsemane, but ultimately he submitted to the will of his Father. He was able to go through with his mission, because he knew with certainty the final outcome. The letter to the Hebrews exhorts us to "fix our eyes on Jesus, the author and perfecter of our faith, who for the joy set before him endured the cross, scorning its shame, and sat down at the right hand of the throne of God" (Hebrews 12:2). It was the "joy set before him" which enabled him to endure the cross. Jesus was willing to go through with his mission, knowing he would return to his Father. Having come from heaven, he knew it was a place where there was "no more death or mourning or crying or pain" (Revelation 21:4).

Unfortunately, we tend to listen more to the voices of advertising, the media, and social commentators of our times. J. I. Packer puts it well:

For today, by and large, Christians no longer live for heaven, and therefore no longer understand, let alone practise, detachment from the world... Does the world around us seek profit, pleasure and privilege? So do we. We have no readiness or strength to renounce these objectives, for we have recast Christianity into a mould that stresses happiness above holiness, blessings here above blessing hereafter, health and wealth as God's best gifts, and death, especially early death, not as thankworthy deliverance from the miseries of a sinful world, but as the supreme disaster... Is our Christianity out of shape? Yes it is, and the basic reason is that we have lost the New Testament's two-world perspective that views the next life as more important than this one and understands life here as essentially preparation and training for life hereafter.

It's important to note in the above that Packer is redressing an imbalance which he observes in many of us nowadays. I've done the same in this chapter as a whole. But we mustn't create a false dichotomy and swing too far the other way either, ending up "so heavenly-minded that we're no earthly good". As the Christian Aid motto states, "We believe in life *before* death." Jesus provides not only hope for the after-life, but hope through our day-to-day trials, challenges, disappointments, and hurts. This is a critical point, which is the meat of Part Three, hence not dwelling on it here.

Our finite minds are bound to struggle to imagine this eternal aspect, which simply doesn't fit into our known time/space paradigms. Neither are stereotypes of playing harps on fluffy clouds conducive to increasing in us a desire to speed our graduation to glory. But when we become fully alive, in the next life, things will be altogether different and more wonderful. I love Willard's description of our future destination. He observes, "We shouldn't think of ourselves as destined to be celestial bureaucrats, involved eternally in celestial 'administrivia'. That'd be only slightly better than being caught in an everlasting church service. No, we should think of our destiny as being absorbed in a tremendously creative team effort, with unimaginably splendid leadership, on an inconceivably vast plane of activity, with ever more comprehensive cycles of productivity and employment. This is the 'eye hath not seen, neither ear heard' that lies before us in the prophetic vision of Isaiah 64:4."

We also have a defective view of how rewarding transitory pleasures on earth are, as well as how entirely other-and-beyond in terms of beauty and magnificence our eternal destination will be. As C. S. Lewis writes, "Indeed, if we consider the unblushing promises of reward and the staggering nature of the rewards promised in the Gospels, it would seem that our Lord finds our desires not too strong, but too weak. We are half-hearted creatures, fooling about with drink and sex and ambition when infinite joy is offered us, like an ignorant child who wants to go on making mud pies in a slum because he cannot imagine what is meant by the offer of a holiday at the sea. We are far too easily pleased."

The Old Testament saints listed in Hebrews 11 lived by faith in this wonderful future promise. They understood that their lives of faith were a journey towards a new and better land: "They did not receive the things promised; they only saw them and welcomed them from a distance. And they admitted that they were aliens and strangers on earth. People who say such things show that they are looking for a country of their own. If they had been thinking of the country they had left, they would have had opportunity to return. Instead, they were longing for a better country – a heavenly one. Therefore God is not ashamed to be called their God, for he has prepared a city for them" (Hebrews 11:13–16).

Living in the light of this glorious hope means our important decisions are made with eternity in view. As sojourners, we travel light. We don't let ourselves become consumed by the fickle fashions and fads of contemporary society. We streamline our spending of time, money and energy. We "throw off everything that hinders and the sin that so easily entangles" and we "run with perseverance the race marked out for us" (Hebrews 12:1). We recognize that our goals and aspirations are altogether different from the short-termism of those who believe they only have this life to live for. "They do it to get a crown that will not last; but we do it to get a crown that will last for ever" (1 Corinthians 9:25). Radical amendments to our lifestyles come out of the glorious realization that a renewed creation is our eternal destination.

A future as supermodels!

Part of our glorious hope is that we'll be given new bodies. If like myself, you have constant niggling physical ailments, then we can rejoice that our body, although "sown in weakness...is raised in power; it is sown a natural body, it is raised a spiritual body" (1 Corinthians 15:43–44). My bad back, dodgy ankles, allergies and asthma will be things of the distant past. We have the certain hope that Christ "will transform our lowly bodies so that they will be like his glorious body" (Philippians 3:21). "And just as we have borne the likeness of the earthly man, so shall we bear the likeness of the man from heaven" (1 Corinthians 15:49).

A physically decrepit F. B. Meyer penned these words shortly before he died, which were subsequently delivered to a friend: "I've raced you to heaven. I'm just off. See you there, Love F. B." He exhibited absolute confidence in his future hope, and longed for his own new imperishable body. When the famous 19th century preacher William Haslam was conducting a service one day, he was summoned by a message which said, "Father's dying and does so want to see you. Will you come?" Arriving at his father's house, he was told, "It's too late. Your father's dead." But he approached his father and spoke tenderly about the loving kindness of the Lord. His father smiled dreamily at the name of Jesus and said, "Not dead, just beginning to live." They were his last words.

As a child I went to boarding school, and so sometimes went months without seeing my parents or going home. When holidays began after the end of a long term, the feeling of anticipation of going home and being with loved ones was tantalizing and euphoric. In C. S. Lewis' words, this is a glimpse of the everlasting joy we'll have when we end our earthly lives. In *The Last Battle*, he wrote, "The term is over, the holidays have begun. The dream is ended, this is the morning. All their life in this world...had only been the cover and the title page. Now at last they were beginning Chapter One of the Great Story which no-one on earth has read, which goes on forever, in which every chapter is better than the one before."

Again with reference to Bonhoeffer, it was his supreme hope in an eternity with Christ which led to his willingness to lay down his temporal "tent" and be executed. As the Nazi soldiers led him away to his execution, he calmly said to them, "For you, it's the end. For me, it's the beginning!"

The comfort of being a stranger

Responding to the call to radical living involves radical hoping. We have a glorious hope which increases our anticipation of what's to come. It puts into context our trials and suffering. We're "God's elect, strangers in the world" (1 Peter 1:1). Why are we described as aliens or strangers? Because here is not home, although the temptation is to live as if it is, becoming overly attached to "stuff" which we won't be taking with us on our last great journey. That's why, however strange it might sound, there *is* comfort in being a stranger. Being a stranger routinely implies being far from home, having limited rights, experiencing fear, prejudice and rejection. The last word to use in conjunction with "stranger" would be "comfort", surely? But no, the comfort comes from the fact that we truly belong to a far better place. For the followers of Jesus, "our citizenship is in heaven, and we eagerly await a Saviour from there, the Lord Jesus Christ" (Philippians 3:20).

Investing in the kingdom of God is the safest risk we can take. We have a guaranteed inheritance "that can never perish, spoil or fade – kept in heaven for [us]" (1 Peter 1:4). C. S. Lewis said, "Anything which isn't eternal is eternally out-of-date." Many aspects of our lives face re-assessing and re-prioritizing in light of this wonderful truth. Such a guaranteed inheritance takes away the fear of the future and conveys a deep-rooted peace and security. What a purpose it brings to our lives! What a privilege it is! Yet with privilege comes responsibility...

CHAPTER EIGHT

High Stakes

> There are only two kinds of people in the end: those who say to God 'Thy will be done' and those to whom God says "Thy will be done".
>
> C. S. Lewis in *The Great Divorce*

Dr Martin Lloyd-Jones, one of the greatest preachers of the 20th century, was a medical doctor before he became a minister. One day he was due to preach at church and was running late. The police flagged him down for speeding. When approached by the policeman, he hurriedly declared, "I am Dr Lloyd-Jones. You mustn't stop me, I'm in a hurry. It's a matter of life and death!"

C. S. Lewis once saw this epitaph on a tombstone: "Here lies an atheist, all dressed up but with nowhere to go." Lewis added his own comment, "I bet he wishes that were so."

Ambushes have been commonplace over the last few years in Burundi, and are an easy way of instilling fear over a whole region. In one such ambush, the rebels ordered everyone out of the bus. In what would seem comical but for the seriousness of what was going on, two people managed to dive into the ditch on the side of the road without the rebels spotting them. One was a huge middle-aged woman; the other, lying face-to-face on top of her in a seemingly highly compromising position, was a pastor. As the rebels lined up the passengers and shot them one by one in the head, the pastor whispered to the woman, "You need to receive Jesus into your heart *right now*, because we're going to die, and you need to know where you're going." Mercifully in this instance they survived to tell the tale.

On another occasion, I was at a crowded meeting near the Congolese border, on a makeshift stage under the blistering heat of the ascending sun. My sermon text was Matthew 25 – the parable of the ten maidservants. In Jesus' story, all of them had been invited to the weddingcelebra- tion. However, as is often the case, the bridal party was late. All the girls nodded off as night fell; but then the call came: the couple were soon to arrive. So the maidservants trimmed their lamps to get ready for the newlyweds. As we know, five maidservants were ready, the other five were not; so the latter had to run off and buy some more oil, during which time the bride and groom arrived. Those ready were welcomed in, and joined the party. The door was then shut, definitively. Those who were late arrived eventually, but were told, "I tell you the truth, I don't know you."

It's a straightforward story, and it doesn't need much explaining. My three points were simply, i) Jesus is coming, ii) nobody knows when, iii) but are you ready? A number of people responded to the invitation. Plenty of others declined. Perhaps some thought they would respond and get themselves ready for next week, or next year. In any case, two days later I was driving towards their village on my motorbike only to be turned back by a group of soldiers, as killing was taking place up ahead in a rebel attack. An undisclosed number died, and it struck me as never before just how urgent a message we have been entrusted with. How many of those who died had accepted or declined the invitation just 48 hours earlier? God knows. For each of those people unfortunate enough to be caught in the crossfire, their time to meet Jesus had indeed come; they hadn't known when; but the most important issue remained the same – were they ready?

Clearly, neither of the above examples is a scenario familiar to many of us. But the same sense of urgency is called for in our respective circumstances if we really understand what's going on around us. The stakes are very high. As John Piper explains, "Most people show by their priorities and casual approaches to spiritual things that they believe we're in peace, not in wartime... In wartime we're on the alert. We're armed. We're vigilant. In wartime we spend money differently, because there are more strategic ways to maximize our resources. The war effort touches everybody. We all cut back. The luxury liner becomes a troop carrier... Who considers that the casualties of this war don't merely lose an arm or an eye or an earthly life, but lose everything, even their own soul, and enter a hell of everlasting torment?"

The desperate reality of hell

The situation is only urgent if we believe what the Bible says regarding the eternal destinies of both the saved and the unsaved. Yet this is one of the most neglected topics, seldom discussed or preached on. The last time I heard a sermon on hell, the preacher said that in his 20 years at that church, he had never heard a sermon on the topic. We can't afford to have a hazy theology of hell if we're to respond to the call to no holds barred discipleship. Hell is relevant to all of us, because it will be the eternal destination of so many people we interact with.

Maybe it seems somewhat grim to enter into this discussion, but it mustn't be avoided. If people choose to bury their heads in the sand and embrace an attitude that ignorance is bliss, we need to open their hearts and minds boldly yet sensitively to see the impending danger. People's natural tendency to avoid facing reality was graphically illustrated on the BA flight 009 from Australia to Indonesia a few years ago. Suddenly, above the Indian Ocean the Boeing 747 began to freefall. The captain spoke on the intercom, "Ladies and gentlemen, this is your captain speaking. We have a small problem. All four engines have stopped. We're doing our best to get them going again. Please remain calm." Charles Capewell and his son noticed smoke in the cabin. The son looked out of the window and saw flames coming from the engine. "Dad, the engine's on fire!" Charles responded, "Well, you'd better pull the blind down and pretend it's not happening."

So this chapter is an attempt to highlight the imminent danger facing many around us – one far worse even than being stuck in a struggling aircraft. The previous chapter dealt with the glorious hope of those who have trusted Jesus for their salvation. It's a certain and living hope, a guaranteed inheritance, "kept in heaven for [us]" (1 Peter 1:4). But the flip side is likewise a reality, i.e. the desperately serious state of those who choose to reject God's offer of forgiveness and eternal life through Jesus. Radical living will involve an undiluted and unequivocal acceptance of the unpalatable doctrine of hell.

There's significant controversy and debate amongst evangelicals as to the dynamics of hell, which won't be addressed here. Below is a limited sample of the many verses from Scripture on the subject.

The Sermon on the Mount is the first recorded instance of Jesus' talking about hell. In Matthew 5:22, he warns us of the "danger of the fire of hell". Verses 29 and 30 reveal that it's "better to lose one part of your body than for your whole body to be thrown into hell." Similarly in Mark 9:47–48 Jesus warned his listeners, "It is better for you to enter the kingdom of God with one eye than to have two eyes and be thrown into hell", where "'their worm does not die, and the fire is not quenched.'" In the parable of the sheep and the goats (Matthew 25:31–46), we read of Jesus' judging people based on what they've done with the hungry, the thirsty, the naked, the sick and the prisoner. In verse 41, Jesus expresses in no uncertain terms the fate of those who neglected to help: "Depart from me, you who are cursed, into the eternal fire prepared for the devil and his angels." Verse 46 concludes, "Then they will go away to eternal punishment, but the righteous to eternal life."

Jesus' parable about the rich man and Lazarus in Luke 16:19–31 makes several points. The rich man in hell is "in torment" (verse 23). He cries out for pity because he's "in agony in this fire" (verse 24). His pleading to enable his family to know about the reality of the torments of hell is denied. As with the foolish maidservants, it's too late. There are no second chances. His family members will either listen "to Moses and the Prophets" (verse 31) or face the same judgement. There's no hint of an end to the conscious torment which the rich man is enduring.

Jesus said that "whoever believes in the Son has eternal

life, but whoever rejects the Son will not see life, for God's wrath remains on him" (John 3:36). In 2 Thessalonians 1:8–9, Paul wrote, "He will punish those who do not know God and do not obey the gospel of our Lord Jesus. They will be punished with everlasting destruction and shut out from the presence of the Lord and from the majesty of his power."

The book of Revelation has two particularly significant passages. In 14:9–11 we read, "A third angel followed them and said in a loud voice: 'If anyone worships the beast...he will be tormented with burning sulphur in the presence of the holy angels and of the Lamb. And the smoke of their torment rises for ever and ever. There is no rest day or night for those who worship the beast and his image, or for anyone who receives the mark of his name.'" Revelation 20:10, 15 says, "And the devil, who deceived them, was thrown into the lake of burning sulphur, where the beast and the false prophet had been thrown. They will be tormented day and night for ever and ever... If anyone's name was not found written in the book of life, he was thrown into the lake of fire."

Theologians throughout the centuries have tried to comprehend and communicate as clearly as possible what they perceive these verses entail. Martin Luther used vivid and frightening language to convey his understanding of hell, saying, "The fiery oven is ignited merely by the unbearable appearance of God and endures eternally. For the Day of Judgement will not last for a moment only but will stand throughout eternity and will thereafter never come to an end. Constantly the damned will be judged, constantly they will suffer pain, and constantly they will be a fiery oven, that is, they will be tortured within by supreme distress and tribulation."

Jonathan Edwards in his much-publicized sermon, "Sinners in the Hands of an Angry God", called out to each member of his congregation, "O sinner! Consider the fearful danger you are in: it is a great furnace of wrath, a wide and bottomless pit, full of the fire of wrath, that you are held over in the hand of that God, whose wrath is provoked and incensed as much against you, as against many of the damned in hell. You hang by a slender thread, with the flames of divine wrath flashing about it, and ready every moment to singe it, and burn it asunder."

Berdyaev describes hell as "the state of the soul powerless to come out of itself, absolute self-centredness, dark and evil isolation, i.e. final inability to love. It means being engulfed in an agonising moment which opens upon a yawning abyss of infinity, so that the moment becomes endless time. Hell creates and organises the separation of the soul from God, from God's world, and from other men. In hell the soul is separated from everyone and everything".

However hard it is to discern between what are pictorial images in Scripture and what are literal descriptions of future realities – quite apart from theologians' interpretations – what becomes abundantly clear is that hell is the most fearful concept. Scripture speaks of hell as a foul place of suffering, frustration, weeping, gnashing of teeth, restlessness, fire, punishment, wrath, torment, shame, darkness and separation. Our minds can't possibly expect to fully comprehend the horrific nature of this desperate place, but we must resist the temptation to dilute our message to make it more palatable for those around us. Responding to a question on the eternal destiny of the unredeemed, leading evangelical apologist Francis Schaeffer simply bowed his head and wept.

All the time in the world?

There's a pithy parable about the devil's training academy for his demonic minions. On the day of the graduation ceremony, he was mingling with the new graduates and questioning them about what they had learnt. He approached one group of three demons and engaged them in conversation. He asked them, "Now that you're ready to start your mission of leading as many earthlings away from the path of God and into my clutches, what strategy will you use?"

The first demon replied, "Sir, I'll tell them there's no God."

"Rubbish! That won't work. Creation's so beautiful that it points to the fact that surely there is a Creator. You won't dupe many with that one."

The second one replied, "Sir, I'll tell them that there's no judgement."

"No chance! Come on, we all know that those pathetic earthlings have been endowed with a conscience so that they inherently have a conception of right and wrong. Most know and recognize a coming judgement. That's not going to work."

Finally, the third demon replied, "I'll tell them that yes, there is a God, and yes, there is a judgement, but also that there's still plenty of time."

"Excellent! You've studied well. Many will be suckers for that lie. Get to it!"

Satan is described in the Bible as "the father of lies", who "was a murderer from the beginning", and when "he lies, he speaks his native language, for he is a liar" (John 8:44). He is a thief who "comes only to steal and kill and destroy"

(John 10:10). He "prowls around like a roaring lion looking for someone to devour" (1 Peter 5:8). He has sought to deceive from the very beginning when he led Eve astray. In turn, all who serve him will speak the same deadly language with the same motivation and the same cunning. Hence the British witch Gerald Broussay Gardner was being cunningly candid when he said, "The witch wants quiet, regular, ordinary good government with everyone happy, plenty of fun and games, and all fear of death being taken away." Why do witches want that? So that people will avoid confronting the most important question of their lives – the eternal destiny of their souls.

A number of years ago, I came across this obituary: "Died, Salvador Sanchez, 23, World Boxing Council feath-erweight champion and one of the sport's best fighters; of injuries after his Porsche 928 collided with two trucks, just north of Queretaro, Mexico. A school dropout at 16, Sanchez explained, 'I found out that I liked hitting people, and I didn't like school so I started boxing.' A peppery tacti-cian, he wore opponents down for late-round knockouts. His record: 43-1-1. 'I'd like to step down undefeated,' he said last month. 'I'm only 23 and I have all the time in the world.'"

Like many young people, Sanchez considered himself practically immortal. Siegfried Sassoon once said, "At the age of 22, I believed myself to be inextinguishable." Actually, so did I. And such an attitude is representative of many for whom old age seems miles away. But it's danger-ous to live that way. Whereas life is uncertain, death is sure. David was right when he said to Jonathan, "As surely as the Lord lives and as you live, there is only a step between me and death" (1 Samuel 20:3). I look back at a number of school friends who have died in the last few years, all of them virile and robust men in their teens or twenties from highly affluent and privileged backgrounds – we are far from immortal – and so we need to be ready.

A friend of mine called Deo spent two years sick in hospital. One night he was woken up by persistent knocking on his door at 3am. A woman needed help to lift her husband to the toilet. Deo was feverish himself, but he crawled out of bed and lugged the man to and from the lavatory. But before going back to bed, he asked the man if he could return in the morning to tell him about Jesus. The man replied, "No. If you want to tell me about Jesus, tell me right now, because I might be dead by morning." Deo spoke of the tender love and mercy of God, and the woman watched as her husband prayed with Deo to receive Christ as Lord and Saviour. In the morning he was dead. But at least he was ready.

Another man who was ready was Charles. Four years ago, this SU volunteer was returning from a wedding when the rebels stopped the van he was in. He was taken to the side of the road with six other men and shot dead. His crime was that he was from the "wrong" tribe. For everyone who loved him, it was a tragedy; but here at least was a man who clearly knew that his citizenship was in heaven, that he had been saved by grace, and that Jesus had paid the price for his sins. That was comforting to us. However, my thoughts immediately moved on to those six other men. Were they ready? Because if not, then their eternal destinies were sealed the moment the shots rang out; and as the verses we've considered above reveal, that's unimaginably grim.

Such examples may seem a long way away from us at work or play, and yet we're all surrounded by people who are living either ignorant of or consciously disregarding this most fundamental issue. As a school friend once said to me, "Maybe I'll think about it when I'm older, but for now I just want to sow my wild oats and have a good time." What shortsightedness! Just across our street, or across the office floor, or across the shopping aisle, people are living by a thread. And for many of us, it takes events such as the Asian tsunami, the belated screeching of brakes as a car accident kills a loved one, or the results of medical tests showing signs of a cancerous growth, to wake us up from spiritual blindness or apathy. Truly, life is precious.

Preaching to the converted

In addressing this most sombre and unpalatable of biblical doctrines, we're not advocating preaching hellfire and damnation to all and sundry. Stereotypes of street preachers ranting at passers-by with a glint of terror (or pleasure) in their eyes don't help our cause. I myself have occasionally done some preaching on the streets, and the challenge for all who try this entirely valid avenue of outreach is how to communicate the whole truth lovingly. It's hard (but not impossible) to shout in love! Communication is what people hear, not necessarily what is said. I may be shouting about the love and mercy of God but conceivably all that the passers-by assimilate are the rants of a deranged and agitated fruitcake! So it's worth considering Jesus' example to see how he reached out to the lost. For a few of us this will be valuable for the context of street-preaching (and Jesus did a lot of that), but for most of us it will apply more generally to reaching out to loved ones, colleagues and the various people with whom we come into contact in our daily lives.

If you read through the gospels, what quickly becomes apparent is that Jesus is not shy of discussing the issue of hell. However, when he does so, it's invariably believers that he's addressing, not "sinners". He spoke of grace to the publicans and sinners, and reserved his strongest and most colourful depictions of hell for those who should have known better. So he taught both grace and judgment, both heaven and hell. The Pharisees had missed the whole message of grace, and in fact showed no gratitude towards their Lord. Rather, in self-righteous complacency, they rested on their laurels, falsely assuming their good works would guarantee an elevated position in heaven.

When dealing with "sinners", Jesus' approach wasn't to dangle them over the pit, or scare them into the kingdom. So Pawson suggests the need "to *see* sinners in this danger, but not necessarily to *tell* them". Similarly, it's better for the follower of Christ "to have hell more frequently in his heart than on his lips. This will fuel his (the believer's) fervency and increase the urgency of his appeal". Pawson himself is a staunch advocate of the traditionalist view of hell as conscious eternal punishment, so he's by no means implying that we should water down the truth. Rather, he's analyzing Jesus' example and seeking to apply it to the preacher's or layman's ministry.

Otherwise – and history is replete with such examples – people can be turned away from the Good News for ever. Many of us have come across folks who have shared their personal horror stories of being the victims of over-zealous and insensitive (albeit perhaps well-intentioned) Christians.

One of the world's richest families in the 19th century

came from Scotland. The Carnegies had extraordinary wealth, and their philanthropy was almost unparalleled in their day. Andrew Carnegie was taken as a child by his father William to the local Presbyterian church in Dunfermline. But William was so appalled at the apparent relish and enthusiasm of the minister in expounding the doctrine of infant damnation that he jumped up and interrupted the unsuspecting preacher. Trembling with outrage, William declared, "If that be your religion and that your God, I shall seek a better religion and a nobler God." William shook the dust off his feet and never again set foot inside another church, resolving instead to bring up his boy as an avowed sceptic. By default, scepticism assumed the place of the "better religion" William had sought. Concerning the "nobler God" he had spoken of, the course of his own life, that of his sons and many others whom they impacted by their generosity could have been so very different had William Carnegie been presented with a forgiving and gracious One.

The Gospel is the greatest news in the world. But it only becomes good news once we have dealt with the bad news; and maybe you can only realize how good the good news is in light of how bad the bad news is. The concept of hell is so desperately bleak that we must be willing to be broken by it, and pray with Frank Laubach, "Lord, forgive us for looking at the world with dry eyes."

Robert Murray McCheyne was a young Scotsman who died in his prime, aged 29, but not before shaking his beloved homeland. Many people wanted to know the secret behind his spiritual power. One such enquirer embarked on a pilgrimage to McCheyne's church, and asked the sexton, "Would you mind telling me what was the secret behind

Robert Murray McCheyne's work?" So the sexton led him into McCheyne's former study and invited him to be seated in the great man's chair. The sexton then said plainly, "Now drop your head on that book and weep, for that's what Robert Murray McCheyne always did before he preached."

My grandfather was a deeply committed, passionate radical for Jesus. He spent 40 years in Africa, experiencing the East African revival first hand as he built the best school of its time in Rwanda, founded the national Scripture Union movement, and translated the Bible into the local language. At his funeral, the speaker said of him, "Peter Guillebaud worked as if he would live forever, and he lived as if he would die tomorrow." My grandfather knew the stakes were high, and he wanted to do all in his power to rescue as many people as possible. His belief in the uncomfortable topic of this chapter underpinned so much of what he sought to accomplish. And in turn for each one of us, the awareness of the reality of hell will deepen our sense of gratitude to God for sending Jesus to die in our place; it will increase our compassion for the lost; it will heighten our urgency in communicating the gospel; it will sharpen our intercession; it will stir up a righteous hatred of sin; it will spur us on in prioritizing mission and evangelism. All these things are integral in the call to radical living and no holds barred discipleship.

Part Three:

No Holds Barred Discipleship –
What will radical living look like?

CHAPTER NINE

Dreamers of the Day

Anything is possible
But he who walks there now
Will have to dream it stubbornly.
                    Anna Akmatova, "Poem Without a Hero"

A certain man was taken by his friend on an exploratory drive outside the city away from where anybody lived. They left the main road and drove on a while until they found a secluded and seemingly insignificant expanse of land. A few tired shacks remained, and some animals grazed peacefully. The friend, Walter, turned off the engine and got out of the vehicle. He started visualizing and describing the incredible plans he had to develop the area. He was offering his friend Arthur the opportunity to buy the surrounding land and make a killing in the process.

But to Arthur it seemed ludicrous. He questioned Walter, "Who on earth is going to drive 25 miles into the middle of nowhere for this absurd project? The logistics of the venture are mind-blowing."

Walter explained to Arthur, "I can take care of the main project myself. But it'll use up all my money. This land bordering it, where we're standing now, will in just a couple of years be jam-packed with hotels, restaurants and convention halls to accommodate the people who'll come to spend their entire vacation here at my park. I want you to have the first chance at this surrounding acreage, because in the next five years it'll increase in value several hundred times."

Looking back on the offer, Arthur reminisced, "What could I say? I knew he was wrong. I knew that he had let this dream get the best of his common sense, so I mumbled something about a tight money situation and promised that I'd look into the whole thing a little later on."

As they returned to the car, Walter sighed and warned Arthur, "Later on will be too late. You'd better move on it right now."

And that's how Art Linkletter missed out on the opportunity to buy up all the land that surrounded what was to become Disneyland. His friend Walt Disney tried to talk him into sharing the dream, but Art thought he was crazy.

A little Disney dreaming...

Walt Disney was clearly a remarkable visionary. His creativity, pro-activity, foresight, drive, determination and persistence were just some of his many attributes. When asked about the secret of his success, Walt replied: "Somehow I can't believe that there are any heights that can't be scaled by a man who knows the secrets of making dreams come true. This special secret, it seems to me, can be summarized in four Cs. They are curiosity, confidence, courage and constancy, and the greatest of all is confidence. When you believe in a thing, believe in it all the way, implicitly and unquestionably."

Board meetings with Walt were legendary affairs. During the early days when Disney's success was far from guaranteed, there were tough decisions to be made. Walt would occasionally spring a new apparently far-fetched and extravagant idea he was planning. Nearly all the board members thought he had gone mad and that he was foolishly risking financial suicide. They gulped and stared at him in astonishment; and that was precisely the desired reaction – it was only when almost every member resisted his idea that he thought it was a big enough challenge to take on! The rest is history. Disneyland and then Disney World became hugely successful realities, although Walt died before the latter was completed. However, at the opening ceremony of Disney World in Florida, the presiding speaker said, "I wish Walt could've seen this!" Behind him, Walt's wife whispered, "He did!"

Now although Disney's confidence was in himself rather than in God, he has much to teach us. The strength of conviction and depth of faith he exhibited are desperately needed in our own lives and in the lives of our churches today. When Jesus died on the cross and rose from the dead, he demonstrated that the impossible had become possible. He said to his disciples, "With man this is impossible, but not with God; all things are possible with God" (Mark 10:27).

You and I, we follow the God of the impossible. For me, a mere man, with all my hang-ups and weaknesses, my dreams will be impossible to fulfil. But not for God – with him all things are possible! So we have a realistic vision of who we are, but also a real vision of who the *Lord* is. As my granny used to say to me, "Even if it's just you and God up against everyone else, you're the winning majority!" And he calls on us to be visionaries, to dream dreams, and to live them out. However, although we sing and declare great truths about the Lord in our meetings and services, although we pay mental assent to the power and might of our awesome God, the reality is that we invariably leave at the end of the service and retreat to lives of suppressed or even absent dreams.

Have you heard the parable of the waddling ducks? In a certain town of ducks, each Sunday morning all the ducks waddle out of their homes and waddle down the road into church. They waddle towards their favoured pews and sit down. The duck choir waddles in and performs a few duck songs, before the pastor duck waddles to the pulpit and delivers a thundering exhortation: "Dear ducks, God has given each one of us wings! These wings enable us to fly. Yes, we can fly anywhere, anytime. Our Scriptures even tell us we can soar on wings like eagles. Nothing can hold us back. So let's get out there and fly!" The gathered congregation of ducks give a hearty "Amen!"...and then waddle home.

Don Quixote's vision in the musical *The Man from La Mancha* echoes that of Walt Disney. As Don Quixote stands with his armour-bearer Pablo Sanchez, they observe a run-down shack in the distance. Don Quixote describes in extravagant terms the grandeur of the elegant castle which lies ahead of them. But Sanchez simply sees a run-down shack, and says it as he sees it. Don Quixote interrupts him sharply: "Stop! Stop right there! I won't allow your facts to interfere with my vision!"

Helen Keller was both blind and deaf, but those limitations didn't constrain her from making a powerful impact on the lives of many. On one occasion she was asked in an interview if there could be anything worse than being blind. She replied, "Oh, yes! There is something worse than being blind. It's being able to see and not having any vision." Poor eyes may limit our sight, but worse than that, poor vision will limit our deeds.

Dreams by definition are not (yet) reality. To see them fulfilled will take perseverance, sacrifice, and commitment. They won't come into being without huge effort. But we must dream, we must have vision, and we must dare to imagine what might come into being if we truly sought to live a radical life of obedience for Jesus. For that's what he's worth. So let's resolve to embrace a life of determined dreaming.

Determined dreaming

I am determined to contribute to my dream of seeing Burundi transformed to lasting peace through a new generation of Spirit-filled, God-fearing men and women of integrity and passion for Jesus. It's a huge dream, and one that humanly speaking is most unlikely. But for God, nothing's impossible, and I've repeatedly seen the power of the gospel at work redeeming "impossible" situations. Many of us are praying to see this dream come to fruition, and there are some remarkably encouraging signs. I'll give you one example: in 1999, a rebel soldier of ordinary rank was shot by the national army in a jungle attack and left for dead by his fleeing companions. He says that he was sure he was going to die, but somehow pulled through after four months of being at death's door. During that time, he had a powerful encounter with Jesus. Then a pastor came and prophesied over him that one day he would become president of Burundi. Well, just a few months ago, that ordinary rebel soldier was elected in democratic elections as president of

Burundi! Can you get excited with me?! Now whether he stays on track, or subsequently gets killed or corrupted, it's hard to deny that God is on the move and playing his part in response to the years of intercession arising from this blood-stained nation.

How about you – what's your dream? Think about it. Crystallize the vision. Seek the Lord. We need to know what we're aiming at, and we need to be alert to seizing opportunities as they arise. If we aim at nothing, we're sure to hit it. If we aim at everything, we're sure to miss most of it. We want to be proactive, rather than waiting passively for circumstances to dictate the course of our lives. Those who wait to be acted upon will indeed be acted upon. So let's be awake, alert, and on the ball. Lawrence of Arabia said, "Everyone dreams, but not equally. Those who dream by night in the dusty recesses of their minds wake up in the day to find it was vanity. But the dreamers of the day are dangerous people, for they may act out their dreams with open eyes to make it happen." Douglas Everett said much the same thing: "There are some people who live in a dream world, and there are some who face reality; and then there are those who turn one into the other." We're not to be daydreamers – because they are liabilities – but we choose to be dreamers of the day, who face reality and transform the present so that it conforms to the likeness of our dreams.

I've listened many times to Martin Luther King's stirring speech on the eve of his assassination. He declared in his own inimitable way, "I have a dream that one day my four little children will live in a country where they will not be judged on the colour of their skin but on the content of their character. I have a dream today!" Yet were I alongside him at the time, just a few decades ago, I would have advised him to moderate his dream, to aim a bit lower, to strive for something more realistic. His dream was simply absurd in the climate of entrenched and institutionalized racism which prevailed in his country. Yet his dream did come true, albeit after his death; and his words ring out with visionary clarity, encouraging other future dreamers to strive for the "impossible", which is rendered possible by the God-of-the-impossible whom we serve.

Another seemingly intractable situation where break-throughs and transformation have proved so elusive is the Sudan, after a civil war lasting decades and costing several million lives. The regime of the North proclaimed *jihad* against the South, seeking to forcefully transform the whole nation and impose Islamic rule. Christians have suffered hugely in the process, with multiple documented instances of people being raped, killed, or kidnapped and sold into slavery. In the midst of such a furnace of suffering, one man preached on Psalm 25, and shared the following message with the assembled worshippers:

Brothers and sisters, the Psalmist says, "to you, O Lord, I lift up my heart..." This today is the prayer of all Christians of all denominations in the Sudan and all Christians all over the world. We're lifting our soul to God because we trust him... Let us stand firm because he is with us. St James says: resist the devil and he will flee. How do we resist the devil who is threatening us today? We heard this morning we don't resist with stones or guns. Our weapon as Christians is the "sword of the Spirit". The Holy Bible and prayer...

I don't want to say bad things, but I must say this: our Lord is powerful. Can anyone tell me of a Christian who took a bulldozer to knock down schools or mosques anywhere? Brothers and sisters in the government, do something to make sure our schools and places of worship are not destroyed. We also assure the government that we won't take up stones or guns to defend our schools or churches.

We know God is in us. We don't fear those who can kill the body. We fear the one who can kill the body and the soul. Continue praying until this issue is resolved. Those who are afraid to die: go home. Because if you are here and one of us dies, you will run away and frighten the rest. We believe God has a purpose in allowing this to happen at this time. It is for the good of Christians this country.

Some people dream of wiping out the Christian faith by the end of the decade. They are entitled to their dream. Let them continue to dream. I have a different dream. I have a dream that the people of Sudan will soon live together in peace and harmony. I have a dream that all the people of the Sudan will be worshipping the one God, the Lord Jesus Christ, by the end of the next hundred years. I have a dream that the Wali, and Turabi, will be the leading apostles bringing the gospel of the Lord Jesus Christ to the people. Are you ready to dream with me?

Are you ready to dream with me? What's your dream? Nourish it, protect it, go for it! Living by faith is about seeing the invisible, and thereby reaching for the impossible. "Faith is being sure of what we hope for and certain of what we do not see" (Hebrews 11:1). That's why "we fix our eyes not on what is seen but what is unseen. For what is seen is temporary, but what is unseen is eternal" (2 Corinthians 4:18). So we who fix our eyes on the invisible are the ones who can do the impossible. If we have big dreams and want to see great changes, we can't aim low, ask for little, or settle for less than the best. Maybe it's a case of going as far as we can see, and when we get there we'll always be able to see farther still. And of course, if it's a big dream, then there will be plenty of objections; but we'll never attempt anything at all if we wait until all possible objections are first overcome.

Clement Stone was a hugely successful financier and philanthropist. He was once asked, "How have you been able do so much in your lifetime?" He replied, "I've dreamed. I've turned my mind loose to imagine what I wanted to do. Then I've gone to bed and thought about my dreams. In the night, I've dreamed about them. And when I've arisen in the morning, I've seen the way to get to my dreams. While other people were saying, 'You can't do that, it isn't possible', I was well on my way to achieving what I wanted."

Dreams bring life, purpose and direction. Without dreams, the soul shrivels. This was graphically illustrated by a study of concentration camp survivors, which aimed to determine the common characteristics of those who didn't succumb to disease and starvation in the camps. The results showed that it was those who retained hope and dreamt against all odds who pulled through. Victor Frankl epitomized such a man. He was a successful Viennese psychiatrist before being incarcerated by the Nazis. Many years later, whilst addressing a number of illustrious dignitaries, he declared, "There's only one reason why I'm here today. What kept me alive was you. Others gave up hope. I dreamed. I dreamed that someday I would be here, telling you how I, Victor Frankl, had survived the Nazi concentration camps. I've never been here before, I've never seen any of you before, I've never given this speech before. But in my dreams, in my dreams, I have stood before you and said these words a thousand times."

Once every aspect of our lives is surrendered to Christ's lordship, then we're ready to dream radically, because those dreams will flow out of a desire and concern to bring glory to him. The bold follower of Jesus recognizes that he's a unique created being, with potential and gifts to be maximized in service for the King; and as the church, we can take note of what the magazine *The Marketing Imagination* says of the future: "The future belongs to those who see possibilities before they become obvious." Knowing that God wants to use us, we choose to seek his face to work out what his will is for our lives, both corporately and individually. We're not naïve or blind idealists, but we work under a different dynamic to our non-believing friends and colleagues, because we follow a supernatural God, "who is able to do immeasurably more than all we ask or imagine" (Ephesians 3:20). So we're not tied down to the accepted patterns or well-worn paths to achieving any given goal, and we can dream big, provided God is behind us inspiring the dream.

One day there will be peace in Burundi. There will be many more casualties as I and others pursue that dream. I hope to be around to see it happen. But whether I am or not, it will most certainly happen! Martin Luther King died in pursuit of his dream. You and I may or may not be called upon to do the same. At any rate, as Langston Hughes said, "Hold fast to your dreams, for if dreams die, life is a broken-winged bird that cannot fly." Many people have given up on dreaming, resigning themselves to safer expectations and more easily attainable goals. Cynicism has superseded and crushed any former idealism or hope of really making a difference. The call to no holds barred discipleship appeals to each one of us to continue to dream; and if our dreams are to come true, they will involve taking risks and stepping out in radical faith. The question is: are you willing to risk acting out your God-given dream?

CHAPTER TEN

A Fair Share

As long as there are people suffering without the basic necessities of existence, to hold onto riches displays an attitude of disobedience to God.   Andrew Kirk

Live more simply that others may simply live.
                                        Christian Aid slogan

Your pockets are full and now you've got to figure out what to spend it on. If you're going to live up to your ideals and your education, it's going to cost you.   Bono

God wants to set his people on fire by his Holy Spirit, not just so that we can arrange church firework displays to entertain the saints, however spectacular they may be. He wants us to share the warmth of that fire with a dying world.
                                        Ross Paterson

To the enquiring crowds who had just been addressed as, "You brood of vipers!", and who desperately sought salvation with the question, "What should we do then?" John the Baptist gave the following answer in Luke 3:11: "The man with two tunics should *share* with him who has none, and the one who has food should do the same" (emphasis mine). Jesus continued this radical teaching in his Sermon on the Mount, and the early church practised it as well. Such pronouncements were not naïve idealism, but practical commands. Radical, yes, but not impossible. Of course, the most vivid demonstration of radical sharing was that of Jesus himself in the incarnation. In Hebrews 2:14, we read that "he too *shared* in their humanity..." The price of his sharing in our humanity was death, but the result of radical sharing is radical fruit, because he died so that "...by his death he might destroy him who holds the power of death – that is, the devil – and free those who all their lives were held in slavery by their fear of death."

The early church is instructive on this issue in a number of ways. Acts 4:32 tells us that "all the believers were one in heart and mind. No-one claimed that any of his possessions was his own, but they *shared* everything they had." What followed? Verses 33–34 show us: "With great power the apostles continued to testify to the resurrection of the Lord Jesus, and *much grace was upon them all*. There were no needy persons among them" (emphasis mine).

The believers were so liberal with their possessions because they knew that their citizenship was in heaven, that Jesus was coming again in judgement, and that it was more important to store up lasting treasures in heaven than self-ishly hoard on earth what would in any case ultimately rot and decay. But can you see the correlation between giving and grace? Was it because the believers were so liberal with their possessions that God was so liberal with his grace?

Faith in action

On many occasions I've been overwhelmed by the sacrificial sharing of destitute believers in Burundi. Some time ago, I drove with a colleague on my motorbike to a displacement camp. It was a very dangerous outing. The rebels had just sent down the chopped-off heads of the soldiers they had ambushed. In vengeful reprisals, the army had killed 40 civilians on their way to the market. There were 40,000 people in the camp, who had been forcibly regrouped several months earlier. They had no electricity, water or sanitation. I was told that ten people were dying day after day, week after week. After the church service, I was taken into a tin shack, and fed beans and rice. I knew this was far beyond what they could afford. They were languishing in misery and starving to death, whilst I would be back in the safety of the capital within half an hour where I could choose from a variety of foodstuffs from my fridge. They were giving me so much out of their so little, as so often we give so little out of our so much.

A Christian trader and a missionary were driving along together. As they passed by a field, the trader observed an old father with his adolescent son dragging a plough painstakingly through the earth. The sight struck him, and he exclaimed, "Wow, these folks are so desperately poor." The missionary replied, "Yes, those two men are believers. During the church building project, they were committed to contributing something towards it, but they didn't have any money. So they sold their one and only ox and gave the proceeds to the church. This harvest they're having to pull the plough themselves." The trader was pensive for a while before commenting, "That really must have been a tough sacrifice." The missionary replied, "Yes, but they didn't call it that, because they considered themselves fortunate to have an ox to sell."

Why is it that, as a general rule, poor people are so much more generous than rich people? Whatever the reasons, we who are wealthy should be challenged by Desmond Tutu's words: "A church that is in solidarity with the poor can never be a wealthy church. It must sell all in a sense to follow its Master. It must use its wealth and resources for the sake of the least of Christ's brethren." Michael Green offers us a yardstick to assess our spiritual progress: "There is one test and one test only of the extent of our love for God and it's a very uncomfortable one: how have we handled the poor?" The apostle James warns us that "faith by itself, if it is not accompanied by action, is dead... Show me your faith without deeds, and I will show you my faith by what I do" (James 2:17–18). Malcolm Muggeridge wrote of Mother Teresa whilst he was searching for spiritual answers to life, "To me she represents essentially love in action, which is surely what Christianity is all about."

Calling for radical discipleship at the Lausanne Congress of 1974, some of the church leaders from Latin America affirmed that "there is no biblical dichotomy between the word spoken and the word made visible in the lives of God's people. Men *look* as they *listen*, and what they *see* must be one with what they *hear*". It's the inconsistencies between words and deeds expressed in Jesus' name by his followers which have so often nullified their intended positive impact.

Throughout the centuries, where Christians got it right, they lived out what they preached; and in turn people observed that their words were consonant with their deeds. Back in the days of the Roman empire, Emperor Hadrian asked Aristides, "Just who exactly are those Christians?" Although Aristides wasn't one of them, he gave the following summary: "They love one another, they never fail to help widows, they save orphans from those who would hurt them. If they have something, they give freely to the one who has nothing. If they see a stranger, they take him home, and they're happy as if he's a real brother."

What a wonderful testimony to the saints of Aristides' day! Unfortunately, such effusive endorsement isn't always the case. A grubby little urchin in the slum was being teased by another boy: "Hah! You say that God loves you. Well, if that's the case, why doesn't he look after you? Why doesn't God tell someone to bring you shoes and a warm coat and better food?" The little urchin thought for a moment. Then, with tears starting in his eyes, he replied, "I guess he does tell somebody, but somebody forgets..."

I don't want to forget. No, I *will not* forget. In our age of easy accessibility to information, "ignorance is bliss" loses its plausibility.

So what does radical sharing mean for us as individuals? The practical outworkings need to be our own. But let's remember that "he who is kind to the poor lends to the Lord, and he will reward him for what he has done" (Proverbs 19:17). What an extraordinary concept, and indeed privilege, to lend to God – with the wonderful accompanying promise of reward!

The rewards will come, but they are conditional too! Romans 8:17 tells us that "if we are children, then we are heirs – heirs of God and co-heirs with Christ, if indeed we *share* in his sufferings in order that we may also *share* in his glory". As Martin Luther King said, "The crown we wear proceeds the cross we bear." We all want the former, but the latter must surely accompany it. Paul prays a bold prayer in Philippians 3:10–11: "I want to know Christ and the power of his resurrection and the fellowship of *sharing* in his sufferings, becoming like him in his death, and so, somehow, to attain to the resurrection from the dead." He's even willing to pray that he might share in the sufferings of Christ, but only because he has a healthy biblical view of what will last, and it's the eternal hope of verse 11 which enables him to endure all the suffering.

Finally, and hopefully obviously, we're called to be radical sharers of the gospel. As Paul said, the root motivation is the love of Jesus: "For Christ's love compels us…" (2 Corinthians 5:14). On 4 July 1854, Charlie Peace was hanged. He was one of London's best-known criminals. As Peace was being led to the gallows, an Anglican clergyman followed him timidly, reading from the Prayer Book, "Those who die without Christ experience hell, which is the pain of forever dying without the release which death in itself can bring." When Peace heard those horrific words, he turned around sharply and shouted in the clergyman's face, "Do you believe that? Do you really believe that?" His surprised victim stuttered and stammered, "Well…I… suppose I do." "Well, I don't," said Peace, "but if I did, I'd get down on my hands and knees and crawl all over Britain, even if it were paved with pieces of broken glass, if I could rescue just one person from what you just told me."

Screaming injustice

On a global scale, poverty is mushrooming whilst affluence is exponentially growing in the hands of a privileged minority – people like you and me. This is a digression of sorts because the emphasis of the chapter is intended to be on our individual lives and actions. However, it's an important digression, because as individuals we contribute to the structural injustices in the world. We can't plead ignorance, impotence or irrelevance. We are part of the system and share in its complicity. Desmond Tutu said, "I am not interested in picking up crumbs of compassion thrown from the table of someone who considers himself to be my master. I want the full menu of rights. If you're neutral in situations of injustice, you've chosen the side of the oppressor. If an elephant has its foot on the tail of a mouse and you say that you're neutral, the mouse will not appreciate your neutrality." The statistics which follow are quickly out-of-date, but they represent alarming trends which are strongly resistant to change.

Ronald Sider's *Rich Christians in an Age of Hunger* makes unpalatable reading for us Westerners, yet it's of paramount importance that we engage with these issues. He notes that "our problem is not primarily one of ethics. It is not that we have failed to live what our teachers have taught. It is that our theology itself has been unbiblical. By largely ignoring the central biblical teaching of God's special concern for the poor, our theology has been profoundly unorthodox... Those who consider themselves most orthodox have fallen into theological liberalism on this issue".

Indeed this issue is so very real to me because in Burundi I'm surrounded by plenty of people who eat one meal a day at best, who can't afford medicine so may die from any innocuous and easily curable disease, who have no recourse to a functional judiciary, who have extremely limited access to education, and negligible career prospects. Most seem condemned to a life of misery, and in many cases only a short life, because of the ravages of AIDS, malaria, famine and war.

Sider quotes a World Bank study, showing that approximately 1.3 billion of the very poorest people on the planet live on less than one dollar a day, with another 2 billion very poor people surviving on less than two dollars a day. Clark Pinnock writes that the story of the rich man and Lazarus "ought to explode in our hands as we read it sitting at our well-covered tables while the third world stands outside". Sider asks us the penetrating question, "Have we allowed our economic self-interest to distort our interpretation of Scripture? But to the extent of our belief in scriptural authority, we will permit painful texts to correct our thinking."

In 1948, Africa's share of global trade was 5.3 percent. By 2002, it had fallen to a wretched 1.7 percent, largely due to the grotesquely unfair trade barriers imposed by developed countries. Experts say that if the continent could regain just an additional 1 percent of global trade it would earn $70 billion more in exports each year – almost six times what it receives in foreign aid. These are issues of injustice. Preventing those at the bottom of the pile from selling their products while we in the "civilized" world sing the virtues of the free market is both outrageous and unjust. Withholding key life-saving medicines out of deference to the Office of Patents is unjust. Holding children to ransom for the debts of their grandparents is unjust. Yes, these are extremely complex issues, but how dare our Western governments constantly claim the moral high ground?

How will future generations look back on a time when many in the West are obsessed with avoiding obesity while much of the developing world doesn't have enough to eat? Africa is hugely dependent on agriculture and has been particularly vulnerable to protectionist farm policies. The appalling Common Agricultural Policy, which combines discrimination against poor countries' exports with dumping of agricultural products in their markets, has wrought havoc. African farmers have seen their livelihoods destroyed. The United Nations estimates that these and other unfair trade practices cost poor countries $760 billion a year. Thirty thousand children die in Africa every day, largely from preventable disease and from lack of food and clean water. So *every week* the equivalent of a 2004 tsunami wipes out African children through disease and malnutrition.

Facts and figures can bamboozle us, but the following are straightforward enough. Sider reports, "A comparison of Western expenditures on foreign aid and the military is startling. In 1991, major aid donors spent 3.55 percent of their GNP on military expenditures but gave only 0.34 percent of their GNP for economic aid. In 1992, world military spending was $815 billion, which was the combined income of 49 percent of the world's people. The level of military spending today is still four times the combined annual incomes for the poorest 25 percent of the developing world's population, the more than one billion poorest people." I've had the unfortunate experience of hearing a sample of those weapons being used for their destructive purposes on a weekly basis, including this morning as I write. The waste of the West is no less sickening: "The dollar value of the food North Americans throw in the garbage each year equals about one-fifth of the total annual income for all the Christians in Africa."

In 1998, a UN Human Development Report said that the three richest people in the world own the amount of wealth equal to the combined GDP of the world's poorest 48 nations. Basic education for the whole world would only cost an extra $6 billion a year, whilst $8 billion a year is spent on cosmetics in the United States alone. Installation of water and sanitation for the whole world would cost $9 billion, but $11 billion is spent on ice-cream in Europe in one year. Healthcare and nutrition would cost $13 billion, but $17 billion is spent each year in the US and in Europe on pet food. $35 billion is spent on business entertainment in Japan, $50 billion is spent on cigarettes in Europe, $105 billion on alcoholic drinks in Europe, $400 billion on narcotic drugs around the world, and $780 billion on the world's armed forces. In 1997, UNDP reports it would cost $80 billion a year to wipe out poverty from the planet until 2007, which is less than one half of one percent of global income and is about the equivalent of the combined net worth of the seven richest men on the earth.

No holds barred discipleship will involve engaging with these issues whilst acknowledging their deep complexities. I can't personally change legislation on Pakistan's blasphemy law, but my campaigning and writing letters will lead to the release of an innocent man accused by a jealous business competitor. I can't dictate the price of coffee on the world market, but I can decide to only buy (and to mobilize others to buy) coffee where guarantees are made about community development for the relevant local producers where the coffee comes from. I'm never going to be a politician, but I can get involved on the board of governors and make sure the local school's Christian foundations and ethos aren't jettisoned in the name of political correctness.

The likes of Wilberforce and the Clapham Group of the late 18th and early 19th century were powerfully used to transform Britain, as they lobbied and campaigned and sensitized people to the social injustices of slavery, factory and slum conditions, and many other important issues. With

God's help they were used to radically reshape and realign British life until every indicator of morality and decency revealed marked improvements: drunkenness, crime, children born out of wedlock, infant mortality, education of the poor, life expectancy – all improved, thanks in large part to the role of passionate disciples who married the need for both proclamation *and* demonstration of the gospel. Wilberforce's catchphrase was "making goodness fashionable", and thus Britain was spared the anarchic events which happened just across the Channel in the French Revolution.

The Reverend Martin Niemöller was a pastor in the German Confessing Church under Hitler. He ended up spending seven years in a concentration camp. His famous words highlight the abject bankruptcy and failure of the church of his day to confront and denounce Hitler's evils: "First they came for the communists, and I didn't speak out because I wasn't a communist. Then they came for the socialists, and I didn't speak out because I wasn't a socialist. Then they came for the labour leaders, and I didn't speak out because I wasn't a labour leader. Then they came for the Jews, and I didn't speak out because I wasn't a Jew. Then they came for me, and there was no one left to speak out for me."

Whereas in the past the church has often failed, the challenge for us in the 21st century is to prophetically call and enact Christ's heart for his precious but degenerate world. The Enlightenment culture has failed to provide solutions, having progressively usurped the influence of the church. The constant compromises of institutional Christianity on issues of biblical truth and morality through the last century have meant that the church has largely abdicated its prophetic responsibility in society. So our role is all the more urgent as we seek wholesale transformation, restructuring and regeneration of spiritually bankrupt individual lives as well as corporate institutions. Christians working in the media, education, politics and the arts all have key roles to play in shaping cultural trends and values. We want to endorse them and support them in their fields, which are uncomfortable and challenging places to act out their faiths, but which are absolutely key in determining where the future goes. It's been done before, it can be done again!

What difference can we make?

In January 2003, I had a life-changing event with a little boy who was dying from AIDS, and I wrote the following:

> Do you know the starfish story? An old man was walking along a beach strewn with thousands upon thousands of starfish that had been washed up by the pounding waves. As he sauntered along, he came across a little boy who was busy picking up each individual starfish and energetically throwing it back into the water.
>
> "Hey, little boy, what are you doing?"
>
> "The sun is warm and the tide is heading out, so unless I hurry, these starfish are going to die."
>
> The old man replied somewhat scornfully, "But look along the shore, there are so many starfish. You will never be able to throw them all back in. You're wasting your time. What's the point? What difference can you make?"

The boy listened respectfully, pondered those words momentarily, and then bent over to pick another starfish up. As he launched it into the air and back into the sea, he triumphantly declared, "Well it made a difference to that one!"

Dear friends,

Well, what difference can we make? Where shall we start? What's the point, with all we're up against? I'm writing this from South Africa, and for three days my life has been consumed with Bongani. You probably know the films *Three Men and a Baby/Little Lady*. For us, it was *Three Men and Little Bongani*. Meet the team:

- Anthony Farr – South African, 30 years old, ex-merchant banker, left his lucrative career because he's a "dreamer-of-the-day", a visionary and a risk-taker, who wanted to move beyond success to significance. So he co-founded "Starfish", with the aim of turning the tide on AIDS in his beloved homeland.
- Peter Barnett – Australian, 31 years old, Rhodes scholar, solicitor, exceptional man and generally good egg.
- Simon Guillebaud – English, 29 years old, just someone wanting to make a difference.
- Bongani – South African, nine years old, dying of AIDS.

The clinic thought Bongani would die last month. But he's scared of dying, and is a stubborn little fellow, so he ate despite himself, regained some strength, and proved them wrong. His fears of death are understandable, having been left traumatized after watching his mum and dad die of AIDS within the space of a few months. He was then taken in by his grandmother. As often happens, a friend's mother recently died. Bongani explained to his friend that "now they are going to take your mum and put her in a dark hole, cover her with rocks and soil, and she will stay there forever all by herself". The little friend cried, and said he wouldn't let them do that to his mum. But Bongani replied, "You can't cry, because that's just the way it is."

Bongani's dream before he died was to go to the coast, play in the sand, and swim in the sea. So we took him to Durban, a six-hour drive from Jo'burg. He was so quiet, withdrawn, skinny and sad. His eyes were initially lifeless, and he was no doubt confused by these three weirdoes who were making ridiculous noises and actions in trying to make him laugh. Slowly but surely he relaxed and loosened up. He stuffed his face when we ate at the service station, and chuckled huskily on the trampoline in the kiddies' play area. Eventually we made it to the beach, and his eyes lit up. We got ready in the car park, and tentatively ventured onto the sand. The waves were huge, so we held him tightly as we paddled into the sea. One crashing wave scared him, and he soon had enough. He remained silent, but the dream had come true.

We spent another two days at God's Golden Acre, a centre where dozens of underprivileged or orphaned kids had been taken in. Bongani never talked, just nodding with his head if we asked him a question. But in the afternoon, I took him to the shallow pool. He gripped me around the neck, but slowly I drew away, and he jumped into my arms. Growing in confidence, he began splashing further from me, and then feigned drowning, saying, "I'm sinking!" That was the first sign of his humour, and his unquenchable little spirit. He was so precious.

On the long drive back to Jo'burg, I lay in the rear of the truck on a mattress, and tried to sleep. Bongani snuggled up sideways to me, and nestled his forehead on my temple as I lay on my back looking at the roof. He slept, and his sporadic sighs occasionally interrupted the more constant snoring emanating from his snotty nostrils. It grew colder as dusk set in, and he clung tight. It broke my heart that my new little friend would soon be dead. Anthony had flummoxed me with the question, "What is God's purpose for Bongani's life?" Can you help me with the answer? One thing I do know is that I'll never forget him.

We dropped him off at school where his buxom granny worked as a cleaner. She had already buried three of her daughters who had died of AIDS. Bongani hesitated in leaving my side, but I pushed him towards her. His sheepish eyes and timid grin were the last I saw of him as we walked back silently to the car, tears flowing on the inside, if not the outside.

What was the point? What difference did that make?

By the year 2010, it is estimated that half, yes *half*, the South African workforce will have been lost to this disease. There will also be *2 million* AIDS orphans. Faced with such facts, we can give up, bury our heads in the sand, or get involved – and that applies to whatever challenge God lays before us. And one by one, bit by bit, we'll get there... His call and challenge to me are in Burundi. For Anthony, they are in South Africa. How about you?

What's he saying? Are you listening? Are you responding?

I never saw Bongani again – he died 18 months later. What was the point of his life? At the very least some of its value can be redeemed if we grasp the above. *We can make a difference!* The needs are everywhere. They may seem totally overwhelming. We may struggle to know where to start. But if we have eyes to see behind the facades of functionality and the superficial veneers of apparent happiness in many of those around us; if we have ears to hear the suppressed sobs of gut-wrenching brokenness and aching loneliness of people in our vicinity; if we have hands to extend and feet to go to those desperately needy for practical help, financial assistance or simply affirmation and affection, then God will use us to make a difference. It could be a few starfish in our own backyard through our own efforts, alternatively it could be a few across the seas in a faraway land through someone else's efforts whom we have financially empowered to go in Jesus' name. I'm so grateful for the fact that the Lord has used many people's generosity to enable me to be involved in the process of throwing back thousands of "starfish" in Burundi, giving them renewed hope, assurance of salvation, healed bodies and souls, or the capacity to make a living and provide for their loved ones – all through Christ's power and for his glory.

God is longing for us to respond to his call to no holds barred discipleship. His plan is to use an all-inclusive community of brothers and sisters who are reckless sharers, selfless helpers, and passionate disciples – who reach out across ethnic, cultural, social, religious boundaries, with love and joy resonating through their every action. Such a community will be one which cares for the body and the soul, for life here as well as life hereafter. It will be uncompromising in holding to what it believes, and sharing its motivation for doing what it does. There are no short cuts or quick fixes. It will take dogged perseverance. We will need to hang on in there through many battles. It'll be a huge challenge. So will we respond to the call? What's it worth?

CHAPTER ELEVEN

Got to Go!

The time for talking is over.

> Emile Leger, upon leaving his Montreal
> mansion to go and live in a leper colony in Africa

The call of God will never take you where the grace of
God will not keep you.

Amy carmichael, a giant of the faith who gave her life in
service of the poor in India, wrote the following from
her precious adoptive homeland:

The tom toms thumped on all night, and the darkness
shuddered around me like a living, feeling thing. I could
not go to sleep, so I lay awake and looked; and I saw, and
it seemed like this:

That I stood on a grassy sward, and at my feet a
precipice broke sheer down into infinite space. I looked,
but saw no bottom; only cloud shapes, black and furi-
ously coiled, and great shadow-shrouded hollows, and
unfathomable depths. Back I drew, dizzy at the depth.

Then I saw forms of people moving single file along
the grass. They were making for the edge. There was a
woman with a baby in her arms and another little child
holding on to her dress. She was on the very verge. Then
I saw that she was blind. She lifted her foot for the next

step – it trod air. She was over, and the children went over with her. Oh, the cry as they went over!

Then I saw more streams of people flowing from all quarters. All were blind, stone blind; all made straight for the precipice edge. There were shrieks as they suddenly knew themselves falling, and a tossing up of helpless arms, catching, clutching at empty air. But some went over quietly and fell without a sound.

Then I wondered, with a wonder that was simply agony, why no one stopped them at the edge. I could not. I was glued to the ground, and I could not call. Though I strained and tried, only a whisper would come.

Then I saw that at the edge there were sentries set at intervals. But the intervals were far too great; there were wide, unguarded gaps between. And over these gaps people fell in their blindness, quite unwarned; and the green grass seemed blood red to me, and the gulf yawned like the mouth of Hell.

Then I saw, like the pictures of peace, a group of people under some trees, with their backs turned towards the gulf. They were making daisy chains. Sometimes, when a piercing shriek cut the quiet air and reached them, it disturbed them and they thought it rather a vulgar noise. And if one of their number started up and wanted to go and do something to help, then all the others would pull that one down. "Why should you get so excited about it? You must wait for a definite 'call' to go. You haven't finished your daisy chains. It would be really selfish," they said, "to leave us to finish the work alone."

There was another group. It was made up of people whose great desire was to get some sentries out; but they found that very few wanted to go, and sometimes there were no sentries for miles and miles at the edge.

Once a girl stood alone in her place, waving the people back; but her mother and the other relations called, and reminded her that her furlough was due; she must not break the "rules". And, being tired and needing a change, she had to go and rest awhile; but no one was sent to guard her gap; and over and over the people fell, like a waterfall of souls.

Once a child caught at a tuft of grass that grew on the very brink of the gulf; the child clung convulsively, and it called but nobody seemed to hear. And the little girl who longed to be back in her gap thought she heard the little cry, and she sprang up and wanted to go; at which her relatives reproved her, reminding her that no one is necessary anywhere – the gap would be well taken care of, they knew. And they sang a hymn.

Then through the hymn came another sound like the pain of a million broken hearts wrung out in one full drop, one sob. And a horror of great darkness was upon me, for I knew what it was – the Cry of the Blood.

Then thundered a voice, the voice of the Lord. And he thundered, "What hast thou done? The voice of thy brother's blood crieth out to Me from the ground."

The tom toms still beat heavily, the darkness still shuddered and shivered about me; I heard the yells of the devil-dancers and the weird wild shrieks of the devil-possessed just outside the gate.

What does it all matter, after all? It has gone on for years, it will go on for years. Why make such a fuss about it?

God forgive us! God arouse us! Shame us out of our
callousness! Shame us out of our sin!

Many Christians nowadays find the above story crude and
offensive, if they even acknowledge any truth in it at all. The
imagery is too vivid and coarse for us because our sensitiv-
ities have been tempered by political correctness and
compromise. But I believe the truth of Carmichael's words
from the depth of my being – be it for far-off supposedly
primitive tribesmen or for self-assured Western sophisti-
cates. The coarse, crude, offensive demonstration of costly
love on the cross was so much more than just a demonstration – it was a terrifying necessity, the ultimate intervention
of a compassionate God, the *sine qua non* which enabled
lost humanity to be redeemed. Such a realization will
propel us into the mission field, far or near, because there's
so much at stake. The apostle Paul's life was never the same
after his interrupted journey to Damascus. From then on,
love for God and for people thrust him out into the world in
Christ's name. He wrote, "For Christ's love compels us,
because we are convinced that one died for all, and
therefore all died. And he died for all, that those who live
should no longer live for themselves but for him who died
for them and was raised again" (2 Corinthians 5:14–15).

As the above verse hammers home, Jesus died for all.
The relevance is for all. The invitation is for all. The urgency
is for all. The call is not for the few. All of us are called to
go. Maybe our question is where, and maybe the answer is
unclear, but we can be sure that God knows and will reveal
his answers to those who seek his face in humble
dependence. So let's step out in faith – let's go to our own
nation, and let's go to the nations.

Going to our nation

We simply have to go, and go in Jesus' name. He commissioned his disciples in Matthew 28:18–20, "All authority has been given to me in heaven and on earth. Go therefore…and lo, I am with you always, even to the end of the age" (New King James Version). But as the quip goes, there's no "lo" without the "go". The promise that he'll accompany us is conditional on our going somewhere that merits his accompaniment. Before his ascension, in Acts 1:8, Jesus declared prophetically, "You will receive power (Greek *dunamis* – from which we get "dynamite") when the Holy Spirit comes on you; and you will be my witnesses (Greek *martures* – from which we get "martyr") in Jerusalem, and in all Judea and Samaria, and to the ends of the earth." So we're told in this verse that we'll be blessed with power from God through his Holy Spirit. But we're blessed in order to be a blessing to other people, not to be self-absorbed, self-preoccupied or self-centred in our receiving of his precious gift.

The church is the one organization that exists to a large extent for those outside of itself. We can't allow ourselves the luxury of playing safe behind closed doors in cosseted pious huddles, immersing ourselves in rapturous worship, assessing the expository skills of the pastor, or getting diverted by inconsequential and peripheral issues whose cosmetic value sucks the very lifeblood of the Body of Christ out of it. The church isn't a building but a living, growing, dynamic, organic movement of Jesus people. And Jesus calls us to go and be his healing hands and feet in a sick and dark world.

It's a mark of quite how dysfunctional much of Western

society is that most of us don't know the people who live on our own street, or in our own apartment block. Such people, whom God has put near to us, may end up living next to us for two decades, and yet never catch the "fragrance of Christ" which we're there to share with them. Our dealings may be limited to a gruff morning greeting as we cross on the stairs, or a cursory acknowledgement on the street as we go past. And two decades or two years later, they know nothing more about Jesus Christ and the hope he offers and yearns to flood into their often mundane, shallow and dreary existence.

That's what "radical going" will mean to most of us. He calls us to go across the street to a lonely neighbour, to go across the office floor to an exhausted colleague, to go across the lecture hall to a disillusioned fellow student, to go into the derelict housing estate to the struggling refugee, to go across the bar or the dance floor to a superficially jovial yet spiritually bankrupt party animal, to go into the marketplace and shopping precinct to those trying to satisfy their emptiness by cramming their lives full of material goods – to appropriate this message which transcends barriers of gender, ethnicity, class and age, and thereby bring meaning and purpose and fulfillment and truth and reality and satisfaction and eternal life to those who are perishing.

I loved my four years at university. I was a zealous Christian hippie on campus. Some people were open to talk about spiritual issues, others were closed. Most ultimately rejected my efforts to share Jesus with them. Maybe they saw my faith as a quirk of my personality. At any rate, opportunities abounded if you looked out for them. All those foreign students were far from home and longing for friendships, but British students were so insular and unfriendly. So any overtures from my side were snapped up. We went out together, chatted about their countries and cultures, their belief systems and aspirations, as well as mine; and through progressively deepening relationships, a number were drawn to Jesus. I had hardly needed to go at all, because these people had *come* – from continental Europe, Africa and Asia.

On Wednesday nights, a small team of nervous students would meet to pray outside the main campus bar and then go in and talk with anybody who was prepared to listen to us about Jesus. It was sometimes great fun, and other times it was painful. One time we came out crying from the aggressive rejection and insults we had received. Another time I came out having had a great laugh, and realizing I had committed myself to living for the coming year with the people I had sat with and only just got to know!

I dreaded Thursday mornings, because that was the one day I had what seemed to me an offensively early first tutorial, at the unearthly hour of 9am! After one such tutorial in the first term, a similarly bedraggled young man asked me back for a "coffee"! As we walked along, he told me that he had seen me in the bar the night before, but there were "so many of those weirdo Christians talking to people" that he had stayed put at his table. He was shocked to hear that I was a weirdo Christian myself! We talked about it, and I declined the "coffee" which, as it transpired, was a joint! He recognized this as a strange meeting, having come from a Christian background, but having rejected Jesus and opted for a promiscuous lifestyle involving drugs and the occult. His parents' main prayer for him, I discovered later, was that he would meet one Christian at university he could relate to, and a fellow hippie had been their answer.

On Easter Sunday 1993, he was prayed over for several hours as demons were cast out and he received total cleansing, freedom, forgiveness and salvation in the powerful name of Jesus. When he bounded up to me at the beginning of the next term, I knew what had happened without him saying a word. Bright eyes and coloured cheeks had replaced his formerly gaunt and wan complexion. He was a new person. As the Bible describes, the old had gone, the new had come (2 Corinthians 5:17). Over successive weeks, he chose to go and share his newfound hope with others on our course. Two of his friends observed the radical changes in him, and decided they wanted the same power in their own lives. Our "going" into the bar to share Jesus was bearing fruit in ways we couldn't have anticipated, planned or imagined.

At my old job, we used to go to the pub and talk about all sorts of things – sex, office politics, money issues, and Jesus Christ! Between us those were the things that we cared about, and so it was natural to talk about them. People were interested and impacted, because they saw Jesus worked in my life, that he gave me meaning and purpose, that he enabled me to avoid the need to get drunk, talk behind people's backs, or try to get one up on colleagues.

Wherever we have lived, Lizzie and I have always invited the neighbours around to get to know each other. Again, most haven't been interested in our relationship with Jesus, but some have. A few have come to church with us, or requested our prayers, and thus far one has come to faith. We're just regular people with an irregular God! Whether we're at school or university, employed or unemployed, mid-career or retired, part of a team or a band or a society – in whatever circumstances and at whatever stage of our lives we're at, he wants us to go, and there's always some-where to go.

I read one morning in the daily devotional *Streams in the Desert*, "Not many of us are living at our best. We linger in the lowlands because we're afraid to climb the mountains. The steepness and ruggedness dismay us, and so we stay in the misty valleys and don't learn the mystery of the hills. We don't know what we lose in our self-indulgence, what glory awaits us if only we had courage for the mountain climb, what blessing we should find if only we would move to the uplands of God. Too low they build who build beneath the stars."

No holds barred discipleship will involve going any-where, be it near or far, convenient or inconvenient, in com-fortable or inhospitable climes. For some, this will mean "going" within our own "Jerusalem", for others it will mean further afield to different "Judea"s and "Samaria"s, and for still others, it will be to the ends of the earth. If that last one is you, don't let anyone stop you. Come out and join in the worldwide harvest. Reject the "sensible" advice and "com-mon sense dictates" of well-intentioned loved ones, because in all probability they simply aren't listening to the Voice who is calling you onwards and upwards. We'll consider "going to the nations" below. But whether it's in your home nation or abroad – the main thing is that we don't stay, hoarding the blessing to ourselves, and preventing others around us from sharing in its immeasurable benefits. *For Christ's sake, let's go!* So I pray for courage for the mountain climb! Will you pray with me?

Going to the nations

When I left the UK aged 25, I didn't know for how long it would be. I was going to a dangerous land, so maybe I would die as one of the many casualties of the protracted war. Or maybe I would live to enjoy my grandchildren. At least I expected to see my homeland again. Such wasn't the case for the regularly newly appointed archbishops of Sierra Leone in the 19th century. When they boarded the ship at Southampton and said goodbye to their loved ones, they knew they would never see them again. They had a life expectancy of just 18 months. Diseases like amoebic dysentery and malaria accounted for most people's lives within a few months of arrival. So these bold and sacrificial missionaries would pack all their belongings in their coffins, knowing the latter would bring their bodies back sometime soon over the coming months or years. What commitment! Lord, make me passionately single-minded in my service of you as those precious servants many years ago!

As I flew to Rwanda and on to Burundi, I took what little money I had with me. But most of it got stolen, so when I arrived in Burundi, I had just a few hundred dollars to my name. It was such an exciting time. God was going to bail me out – I didn't know how, through whom, when or where – but I knew he would, because he had promised to go with me. I had cast my all on Almighty God, and set off on the adventure of living for him.

My situation as a new arrival in Burundi reminded me of a man who set sail across the Atlantic Ocean with 700 men under his command. His name was Cortez, and the year was 1529. Their mission was the conquest of Mexico. So when they disembarked at Vera Cruz, Cortez promptly set fire to his fleet of eleven ships. Then all 700 men watched as their only exit strategy sank in the depths of the Gulf of Mexico. The only course of action left was to press on into the interior and fight for their commander.

In a similar way I had felt the awesome significance of burning my boat back in Britain and arriving in Burundi with the objective of spreading the reign of Christ my commander in that land. There cannot be a bigger privilege than to follow Christ wherever he leads. It may be costly, dangerous, draining, awkward, unpopular, mundane, exciting or exasperating, but it is most certainly a privilege, and not one which anybody will regret embracing.

Last century a young man felt the call of God on his life to go to China. William Borden was an undergraduate at the time. He came from an affluent family and attended the prestigious Yale University. His prospects were as good as anyone's, and a successful career would surely follow in whichever field he set his mind to excel. So his family and friends were horrified when he chose to give up everything and head for China. "If you want to do good things, then surely there are plenty of needs here. Don't waste your life in a foreign country!" they remonstrated with him. But he knew what he had to do. He boarded a ship for China, full of faith and hope. By the time he had reached Egypt, however, it was clear to everyone that he was a dying man. It was at this point that he might have slipped into self-pitying despair. Thoughts could have entered his mind such as, "What a waste of my life! They were right. I should have stayed back home and had a respectable life, enjoying my family and friends." But no, as he lay dying in the port of Suez, he scribbled a brief note to his loved ones in America which made a powerful epitaph – just six words: "No reserve, no retreat, no regrets."

Another young man taken home by the Lord was David Brainerd, who died in 1747, aged 29. He pioneered outreach to the Indians in New Jersey. The last words in his journal as he lay dying were as follows: "Friday, October 2nd: My soul was this day, at turns, sweetly set on God: I longed to be 'with him' that I might 'behold his glory.'... Oh, that his kingdom might come in the world; that they might all love and glorify him for what he is in himself; and that the blessed Redeemer might 'see of the travail of his soul, and be satisfied.' Oh, 'come, Lord Jesus', come quickly! Amen."

John and Mary Ann Paton sailed for the cannibal island of Tanna in 1858. Within a year, Mary Ann and their newborn son died of fever. John Paton buried them alone. He thought he would go mad, but took comfort from the incredible words of his wife before she died: "I do not regret leaving home and friends. If I had it to do over, I would do it with more pleasure, yes, with all my heart." In turn he was able to declare, "Whensoever Tanna turns to the Lord and is won for Christ, men in after years will find the memory of that spot still green, where, with ceaseless prayers and tears, I claimed that land for God in which I had buried my dead with faith and hope."

We may not even live to see the fruit of our endeavours, but like Mary Ann Paton, or David Brainerd, or William Borden, we're not called to success, but to loving, faithful obedience, in the big things as well as in the small things. Mother Teresa of Calcutta was once asked, "How do you measure the success of your work?" She looked puzzled for a moment and then replied, "I don't remember that the Lord ever spoke of success. He spoke only of faithfulness in love. This is the only success that really counts." Indeed God may call us to go to places where "success" won't be immediately forthcoming. Some people groups are very hard to reach for Christ. A missionary who worked for many years among an exceptionally resistant people said, "We're not reaping the harvest; we're not weeding the crop or sowing the seed or even ploughing the soil. We're just removing the stones."

Let's meditate on and ponder such words from former saints who form the "great cloud of witnesses" (Hebrews 12:1) in heaven who are cheering us on to the finishing posts. I feel like I'm on holy ground when I enter into the painful reality of their words, the costly commitment, the anguish and desperate clinging to their sovereign God. *Lord, make me such a man!*

"The nations are not for me!"

What's it worth? That question has underpinned this whole book. When Jesus went to such extremes to rescue a dying world, how far should we go in obedience to him? Is he worth my most, or my all? When he stretched out his hands on the cross, he showed how far he was prepared to go. Does he really want me to be prepared to go that far? If I am honest, the above examples of radical and costly surrender fill me with nervous fear and anticipation – even dread. I struggle to relate to their depth of commitment. I'm not even sure I want to share that depth of commitment. Knowing how inherently fickle and weak I am, I ask myself a number of disturbing questions: will I let him down? Will he call me to pay the ultimate price? Will I be willing to go through with it? Will I stay the course?

In a sense, those questions are unanswerable. But they do force me back to dependence on the grace of God. Only with his help will I make it. We're ambassadors of God's grace, in a world where grace is in short supply. However, most of us at least live in lands where we've heard of this grace, where we've had opportunity to receive this grace. What of those lands where people haven't heard? God's call to no holds barred discipleship and radical living bellows out our commissioning orders to invade such areas with the grace and fragrance of Christ. Yet much of the church is sleeping through the watch, ignoring the urgent instructions to go to all nations. One hundred and fifty years ago, Andrew Murray gave this damning verdict on the problem with the church: "As we seek to find out why, with such millions of Christians, the real army of God that is fighting the hosts of darkness is so small, the only answer is – lack of heart. The enthusiasm of the Kingdom is missing. And that is because there is so little enthusiasm for *the King*."

We want to recapture the fire of Borden, Brainerd and the Patons. We want to echo Count Nicolaus Ludwig von Zinzendorf's words, "I have but one passion – it is he, it is he alone. The world is the field and the field is the world; and henceforth that country shall be my home where I can be most used in winning souls for Christ." Zinzendorf was instrumental under God in sending many Moravians around the world to reach out to the lost. Two such Moravians offered themselves up as slaves for the Americas so as to get free passage on the ship ferrying Africans across the seas. They laboured and suffered and died reaching out to people who would face a Christless eternity if they didn't turn to Jesus.

We simply can't reject God's call to go to all nations. That doesn't mean we all have to go ourselves. But we're all implicated, and we must all get deeply involved – giving sacrificially, praying strategically, sending and supporting closely those on the front line. There are still around 1.5 billion people who haven't had the chance to hear about Jesus. Only 2.5 percent of missionary effort is expended on these people. We must educate our own people in our congregations, and determine to be involved in changing the nations and speeding Jesus' return.

The task may seem overwhelming. So how shall we go about it? We could identify and invest in singles or couples in our churches who are radically surrendered to God, and give them a ten- or twenty-year commitment as we identify together an unreached people group and work towards the goal of their going with the light of Christ and penetrating the dark satanic strongholds with the gospel message. We could get behind the most gifted and zealous local believers and empower them through our finances to reach out far more effectively and cheaply than what can be achieved through the lengthy process of sending one of our own cross-culturally. We can harness and maximize the potential of radio and the internet, translation of materials into indigenous languages, and printing of literature. All of these cost money, so if we're desperate for the Kingdom rule of Christ over the nations, it will require a mass mobilization of the people of God to go themselves or empower others to go through whichever means are available and relevant to any given context.

Many of us watched in horror as the twin towers of the World Trade Centre crumbled to pieces, killing many innocent people. Yet every day, as John Zumwalt notes, the equivalent of fourteen towers collapse as 50,000 people die among the unreached of our world without ever having heard of Jesus; and Jesus watches them with the same horror that we felt on 11 September 2001. He pleads with us to wake up from our own slumber and wake others up so that we address these issues with urgency instead of casual indifference. If we're disinterested in world missions, it can mean one of only two things: either we're plain ignorant, or we're plain disobedient. God cares so much about the non-Christian world that we can't afford to ignore it.

Can I hear the tom toms still beating heavily? Beyond the fuzzy feelings of fellowship within my network of believers, can I hear the cry of the blood? Am I awake to the oppressive darkness all around me? Can I decipher amongst the competing voices of my frenetic life the distant sound like the pain of a million broken hearts wrung out in one full drop, one sob? We have the keys of the kingdom. Let's use them! It's time to go.

CHAPTER TWELVE

Total Surrender

There are plenty of Christians to follow the Lord halfway, but not the other half. They will give up possessions, friends, and honours, but it touches them too closely to disown themselves.   Eckhart, fifteenth century mystic

If you have to calculate what you're willing to give up for Jesus Christ, never say that you love him. Jesus Christ asks us to give up the best we've got to him, our right to ourselves.   Oswald Chambers

When you surrender, you recognize that you've been defeated. It's a position of weakness, therefore requiring humility. It means that you acknowledge that your rights and welfare are out of your own control. The person to whom you surrender has power over you. You no longer have authority over your own life. You have begrudgingly or willingly laid down whatever weapons or assets were used to resist and defend yourself in the jungle of life. To surrender is to admit powerlessness, and to cast yourself on the mercy of whatever or whoever has defeated you.

Similarly when we agree to a total surrender to the lordship of Christ in our lives, it involves recognition of defeat, admission of powerlessness, acknowledgement of weakness, and humble dependence on the mercy of God. Paradoxically, our waving the white flag of submission to

God's right over our lives is the key that unlocks the gate to many future victories in his name. Yet painful as it is to surrender to Christ, it's our great privilege to do so in service of the King; and the purpose of our surrender is to bring glory to him, who longs to entrust us with the power to accomplish his plans and purposes through us.

So, at the risk of pee-ing you off (!), let's consider five aspects of total surrender: the purpose, power, practicalities, pain and privilege of total surrender. In my own life, total surrender is a distant goal – an ideal, even; and yet that goal or ideal is nearer today than it was yesterday, and by God's grace each one of us will eventually reach that goal as we enter his throne room and bow down before the King of Kings in humble adoration.

The purpose of total surrender

God is glorified as people recognize him for who he is, and give him the praise and adoration that he deserves. So the purpose of total surrender is that our lives will honour him and point others to him. Beyond that, the purpose of total surrender is to bring us to a position of such weakness that we are malleable and available to God to accomplish his purposes for his glory. Paul eventually understood the purpose of weakness before God, when after much pleading over his "thorn in the flesh", he heard God's answer: "My grace is sufficient for you, for my power is made perfect in weakness" (2 Corinthians 12:9). So Paul concluded in that same verse, "Therefore I will boast all the more gladly about my weaknesses, so that Christ's power may rest on me." As we'll see shortly, the result of surrender to Christ is that it unleashes the power of Christ in our lives.

Hudson Taylor was a potent instrument in the hands of God. As founder of the China Inland Mission, he had a profound impact on the lives of many millions of people as he trumpeted the call to penetrate the vast unreached areas of that great nation. He once said, "God chose me because I was weak enough. God doesn't do his great works by large committees. He trains somebody to be quiet enough, and little enough, and then uses him." Well, Lord, help me to be quiet enough, and little enough, and in that position, by your grace, grant me power for your name's sake!

The power of total surrender

Recognized as one of Britain's greatest ever preachers, Spurgeon once wrote, "Give me twelve men, importunate men, lovers of souls, who fear nothing but sin and love nothing but God, and I'll shake London from end to end." The power of a surrendered life is immense, because those who have laid their all on the altar are pure vessels for the ministering of God's Spirit into any given situation. I no longer just possess a faith, but more than that, my faith possesses me.

Walter Lewis Wilson was an American doctor born towards the end of the 19th century. He was a faithful Christian who often hosted visiting missionaries to his church. One visitor from France didn't mince words, asking him, "Who is the Holy Spirit to you?" Wilson's answer was doctrinally correct: "One of the Persons of the Godhead... Teacher, Guide, Third Person of the Trinity." But it was an empty and rehearsed response. His friend pushed him harder, challenging him, "You haven't answered my question." Wilson opened up with real candour: "He's nothing to me. I have no contact with him and could get along without him."

The following year, Wilson listened to a sermon at church from Romans 12 on the challenge to offer his body as a living sacrifice. The preacher called out from the pulpit, "Have you noticed that this verse doesn't tell us to Whom we should give our bodies? It's not the Lord Jesus. He has his own body. It's not the Father. He remains on his throne. Another has come to earth without a body. God gives you the indescribable honour of presenting your bodies to the Holy Spirit, to be his dwelling place on earth."

Wilson was struck to the core and rushed home to seek the Lord. He fell on his face and pleaded with the Lord, "My Lord, I've treated you like a servant. When I wanted you, I called for you. Now I give you this body from my head to my feet. I give you my hands, my limbs, my eyes and lips, my brain. You may send this body to Africa, or lay it on a bed with cancer. It's your body from this moment on."

The next morning, Wilson was working in his office when two women arrived, trying to sell him advertising. He immediately led them to Christ. The previous night's surrender had enabled him to access new power from on high. From that day onwards, his life entered a new dimension of evangelistic fruitfulness. He went on to pioneer a church plant, a mission organization, and a Bible college, as well as becoming a best-selling author.

Do you want to be entrusted with that same power from the Holy Spirit? Well, who is the Holy Spirit to you? Like the early Wilson, can you get along perfectly well without him? Or are you truly willing to offer him your body as a living sacrifice, without conditions or caveats? There's so much more power that I want to plug into for God's glory. But will I trust him for every aspect of my life? Will I "consider everything a loss compared to the surpassing greatness of knowing Christ Jesus" (Philippians 3:8)? These are big, big questions. Here's inviting you to total surrender. If you're ready for it, then how about taking a few minutes and reflecting on John Wesley's "Covenant Prayer", and then making it your own:

> I am no longer my own, but yours.
> Put me to what you will,
> Rank me with whoever you will.
> Put me to suffering.
> Let me be employed for you,
> Or laid aside for you.
> Exalted for you, or brought low for you.
> Let me be full,
> Let me be empty.
> Let me have all things,
> Let me have nothing!
> And now, O Father,
> You are mine and I am yours. So be it.
> And the covenant I am making on earth,
> Let it be ratified in heaven. Amen.

The practicalities of total surrender

In surrendering every aspect of our lives, what do we mean, and what will it look like? Let's take a few examples.

Nobody likes being mocked or marginalized, slandered or scoffed at, be it by colleagues or friends or random people we come across. Well, God wants us to surrender our fear of people, our desire for popularity, and our longing for respect and reputation. He wants us to stand up and be counted, to face the music, to nail our colours to the mast.

Observing one of the pivotal decisions in John Wesley's life highlights the inner conflict that went on as God called him to radically surrender his reputation. His contemporary and friend, Whitefield, had already resorted to preaching in fields and marketplaces, due to the fact that evangelicals were being denied access to more and more pulpits countrywide. Wesley didn't want to preach in the open air, but there seemed little alternative. He went through a time of deep inner turmoil and wrestling. The idea of preaching in the fields was repugnant to him, as to just about everyone else in his day – except Whitefield, who was seeing astonishing results. Gradually Wesley came round to the idea. When a friend remonstrated with him and appealed to him not to soil his good standing in society by stooping to such crude methods, Wesley replied, "When I gave my all to God I did not withhold my reputation." He began preaching in the open air, saying, "I consented to be more vile... I set myself on fire, and people came to see me burn."

God doesn't just want our reputation or desire for acceptance. Another aspect of our total surrender will be our finances. How powerful and liberating it is for those who put this into practice! Jesus in the Sermon on the Mount reassures each person who listens to him, saying, "Do not worry about your life, what you will eat or drink; or about your body, what you will wear... Who of you by worrying can add a single hour to his life?... And why do you worry about clothes... O you of little faith? So do not worry, saying, 'What shall we eat?' or 'What shall we drink?' or 'What shall we wear?' For the pagans run after all these things, and your heavenly Father knows that you need them" (Matthew 6:25–32). The open secret of surrender to God is to "seek first his kingdom and his righteousness, and all these things will be given to you as well" (verse 33).

Sadly, most of us simply can't quite believe that God's Word and promises are totally trustworthy. We need a safety net, a contingency plan to bail us out on the off-chance that he's too busy with other more important business. Or maybe he doesn't really care. Or maybe he just isn't powerful enough. You see, we may not live what we profess, but we will all live what we believe deep down; and we need to be frank about where we're at before being able to move forward. Manning asks provocatively, "When will Christians be honest enough to admit that they don't really believe in Jesus Christ? That the Nazarene carpenter must be dismissed as a romantic visionary, a starry-eyed reformer hopelessly out of touch with the 'real' world of domination, aggression, and power? Only when they realise that they have embraced their culture as their false god!"

As I compare wealthy Western friends with desperately poor African believers, there seems precious little correlation between wealth or poverty on the one hand and happiness or fulfilment on the other. The more you have, the more you think you need. The more you earn, the higher the required standard of living. We think we manage our finances, but the more we accrue, the more they end up managing us. Although people justify the exhausting hours of work by saying the money they earn will allow them to enjoy their leisure pursuits, ultimately they often become enslaved rather than empowered by the money they earn. If that's the case, then their influences and models are clearly not drawn from the Bible, rather from the other rats scurrying around us in this manic life-sapping rat race; and as someone quipped, even if you win the rat race, you're still a rat! But as believers, we're not rats, because our job has a higher and broader purpose – at least it should have – no, it *must* have.

Our colleagues and friends around us can see what really motivates us. And the evangelistic impact of finances surrendered to Christ is seriously underestimated. But again, we let ourselves get squeezed into the world's mould; we "conform...to the pattern of this world", rather than being "transformed by the renewing of [our] mind" (Romans 12:2). As John Piper notes, "The point is: a $70,000 salary doesn't have to be accompanied by a $70,000 lifestyle. God is calling us to be conduits of his grace, not cul-de-sacs. Our great danger today is thinking that the conduit should be lined with gold. It shouldn't. Copper will do. No matter how grateful we are, gold will not make the world think that our God is good; it will make people think that our god is gold."

What would our colleagues or friends answer, if asked what seemed to really matter to us? How we spend our money is one of the clearest indicators. Wesley set a good example in this regard. At a certain point in his life, he decided that a fixed sum was all he needed to live on for a year. He kept to that for the rest of his life. As revenues from books and sermons mounted, and as people confided huge sums of money to him, he could have justified keeping substantially more. But why did he live as he did? Because he was a child of the King, he had a much greater inheritance to come, he recognized his stay on earth wasn't for ever, his citizenship was in heaven, and so he preferred to store up treasures there. In heaven, treasures will *last*. Here they won't. Couldn't you right now as you read just make a quick evaluation of your income, standard of living, needs, wants, expectations, hopes etc., and resolve to live at a specified level for the rest of your life? Then, in ten years' time, when in all likelihood your salary has substantially increased, you won't be tithing (a fair assumption?), but giving much more; and you'll experience the truth of Jesus' words that there is more joy in giving than in receiving.

"How much should we give?" Are we even asking the right question in the first place? The Bible often talks about tithing (mostly in the Old Testament) – but in our hearts are we just trying to give the minimum required? Instead of asking, "How much should I give?" shouldn't we rather be asking, "How much should I keep?"? I met a man in Brazil who was giving 30 percent of his income to the Lord's work, and was aiming to give 90 percent. He observed that the Lord seemed to be blessing his business in a manner commensurate with his generosity. He and his family lived simply, humbly and happily. Isn't that enough for us? I think of a friend who took a massive pay cut to be more strategic in meeting and befriending Muslims in the inner city. Some other friends have given up a big salary and career, and bought up their local pub. They were warned by the previous owner that each morning they should greet the pub's ghost as they opened the curtains – otherwise things would inexplicably go wrong that day. They replied that they were bringing their own ghost, the Holy Ghost, and that there wouldn't be room for both of them! Church now meets there Sunday morning, and many people are enjoying the new atmosphere in that place. Yet those examples are exceptional, because most of us prefer to settle for the security of the suburbs – safer, cleaner, healthier and more respectable. Jesus is our judge, nobody else, so let's evaluate these issues before him alone, in integrity of heart and honesty of motives.

Beyond our finances, God calls us to surrender our agenda and future plans. This surrender is all-encompassing, and involves our career, our desire for a wife or a husband, our desperation and longing to see friends and family members coming to faith, and our fears and insecurities about what is yet to come. So much worry and energy will be spared if we move beyond theoretical assent to practical trust in the Lord for all these areas of our lives.

We'll seek to surrender our use of time, and fight against our careers sucking every ounce of energy and vision out of us to the detriment of investing in people and relationships. We'll avoid becoming enslaved by our schedules. People are more important than programs, and they can quickly tell what matters most to us. As the African said to the Westerner, "You people have watches, but we have time!" Most of the people we work and deal with are crying out for real relationships, for the opportunity to share from their heart with someone who will take the time and desires to listen and not judge. But we're invariably too busy with more "important" things clamouring for our attention.

The practical outworking of our total surrender to Jesus will manifest itself in different ways in our respective situations. But this is no soft sell. It will cost us. It will involve pain. Will it be worth it?

The pain of total surrender

In offering ourselves up as living sacrifices, we die to ourselves – to our right to ourselves. It will undoubtedly be painful, and that pain will be multiplied by being misunderstood by our more respectable brothers and sisters. But we need to remember that the cross was never respectable. It was foolishness, an insult, a shame, a disgrace.

In laying down our right to ourselves, we're casting ourselves on the mercy of God, trusting him for everything, and allowing him to do with us whatever he wants. He's worthy of that trust, and will do what's in our best interests, but that doesn't mean that he'll do things our way. Tozer comments, "Breezy, self-confident Christians tell us how wonderful it is to accept Christ and then have a good time all the rest of your life; the Lord won't demand anything of you. Yes, he will, my friend! The Lord will demand everything of you. And when you give it all up to him, he may bless it and hand it back, but on the other hand he may not..."

I have a friend who prayed that the Lord would do anything in her life to make her more effective for him. The following day she woke up assailed with doubts about the reality of her faith, and has just clung to Jesus for the last decade, still sharing the gospel with many and being used to draw others to him despite her own personal darkness. As I wrote that last sentence, an email came in about a fabulous young missionary who was killed in a car crash in West Africa last night, leaving a wife and three-year-old daughter. They had only been in the field several months after many years of single-minded preparatory training. Try giving a breezy and self-confident answer to those situations, and you're setting yourself up for a fall. I feel bemused, gutted, and angry, even. One day I'll get my answers, but in the meantime I'll have to wrestle with my God whose ways and thoughts are not the same as mine...

So we may not fully understand, but we surrender and submit to the Lord, trusting that he sees the bigger picture. We willingly put ourselves in his vice, on his anvil or in his purifying furnace, and embrace whatever he sees fit to do to us. We cling to the fact that there's a purpose in sufferings and difficulties when they arise. During a weekly Bible study group in Kentucky, the book of Malachi was being studied. In Malachi 3:3, they read, "He will sit as a refiner and purifier of silver." The group discussed this analogy to understand what the significance was. It seemed the Lord chooses to put his people in the furnace; the purpose is to burn off the impurities; God watches the refining process take place; it's a painful process. One woman in the group was fascinated by the analogy and wanted to gain the full impact of it, so she went to see a silversmith in action the following day. She observed him at work for a while, and then asked him, "Do you have to sit the whole time the refining process is taking place?"

"Yes," he replied, "it's crucial – because if the refining process is exceeded by the slightest degree, the silver will be damaged."

The woman was comforted by the thought that similarly the Lord was watching over her, and however difficult her current circumstances were, he was in control. He wouldn't let the refining process go on a minute longer than was required, because his purposes were good, and he didn't want her to be damaged.

The silversmith carried on gazing intently into the furnace. After a further while, the woman got up to leave, but as she was halfway out of the door, he called her back and told her he had forgotten one important detail: *he only knew that the refining process was complete when he could see his own image reflected in the silver.*

So the process of total surrender may be painful. But no pain, no gain! That's hard to accept, as our natural inclination is to avoid pain and opt for the easier road. David Livingstone once received a letter from a society in South Africa: "Have you found a good road to where you are? If the answer's 'yes', we want to send other men to come and help you."

Livingstone replied, "If you have men who will come *only* if they know there's a good road, I don't want them."

I dream of being part of a generation who count the cost and are willing to embrace the pain of surrender. Islam seems to produce tens of thousands of such individuals who understand that victories are costly. In a telling discussion the Ayatollah Fadlallah, spiritual leader of Islamic fundamentalist Hezbollah in Lebanon, said to Brother Andrew,

"You Christians have a problem."

"What do you think our problem is?"

"You're not following the life of Jesus Christ any more."

"So what do you think we should do about that?"

"You must go back to the Book."

Going "back to the Book" will involve re-reading the Scriptures and noticing they are filled with references to the reality of how hard and painful it is to follow Jesus all the way. If we consider just one of Paul's epistles, in 2 Timothy he writes, "Join with me in suffering for the gospel" (1:8); "That is why I am suffering as I am" (1:12); "Endure hardship with us like a good soldier of Christ Jesus" (2:3); "Therefore I endure everything for the sake of the elect"

(2:10); "You, however, know all about my...endurance, persecutions, sufferings... In fact, everyone who wants to live a godly life in Christ Jesus will be persecuted" (3:10–12); "Endure hardship" (4:5). Only a highly selective and blinkered reading of Scripture can produce a working understanding that to come to Jesus is to be spared of any problems, to experience uninterrupted ease and prosperity. There are plenty of wonderful promises for us to take hold of, but only within the context of the Bible as a whole.

So will we get back to the Book, delve deeply into its riches, and live out the message? Salvation was a free gift for us, but bought at great cost by the Lord. Although grace was free, it wasn't cheap. God paid with the blood of his Son on the cross, and we in turn are called to follow. So although the entrance fee is nothing, the annual subscription is everything! Yet however hard it may be at times, we can be assured that after the pain comes the gain.

The privilege of total surrender

The promises of Scripture are so breathtakingly liberating that total surrender becomes the most obvious step in the world. God says he'll never leave or forsake me (Hebrews 13:5). In fact, the one who is in me is greater than the one who is in the world (1 John 4:4). I'm free from any guilt of my past life, because "there is now no condemnation for those who are in Christ Jesus" (Romans 8:1). My old life's gone, I've got a fresh start (2 Corinthians 5:17). I can have absolute certainty about where I'm going, because the Scriptures were written "so that you may *know* that you have eternal life" (1 John 5:13). I'll never lack anything I need, because God will meet all my needs "according to his glorious riches in Christ Jesus" (Philippians 4:19). "I can do everything through him who gives me strength" (Philippians 4:13), so I can dream big dreams and challenge the impossible.

What more could we ask for? We have a fresh start. Our slate has been wiped clean. We have a guaranteed future. We have purpose in the present. We have a privileged position as "heirs of God and co-heirs with Christ" (Romans 8:17 – note how the verse ends though), and Jesus calls us "friends" as opposed to "servants", "because a servant does not know his master's business" (John 15:15). God has "blessed us in the heavenly realm with every spiritual blessing in Christ" (Ephesians 1:3). So as I gaze at Jesus' painfully outstretched arms on the cross, I ask myself: how far is too far when he went that far? As Oswald Chambers said, "Our notion of sacrifice is the wringing out of us something we don't want to give up, full of pain and agony and distress. The Bible idea of sacrifice is that I give as a love-gift the very best thing I have."

C. T. Studd was the best English cricketer of his day, and a man of huge inherited wealth. In the light of what Christ did for him, however, he gave all his fortune away, turned his back on the adulation of his sporting fans, and embraced the privilege of laying down his life in total surrender to Christ on the mission field. He said, "If Jesus Christ is God and died for me, then no sacrifice can be too great for me to make for him." David Livingstone was another man with countless admirers (legitimately so, as he was a fearless and intrepid explorer, as well as a humble man of God). In response to people's extravagant praise and comments to him concerning his "selfless" life, he wrote in his journal, "People talk of the sacrifice I've made in spending so much of my life in Africa. Can that be called a sacrifice which is simply paying back a small part of the great debt owing to our God, which we can never repay? Is that a sacrifice which brings its own blessed reward in healthful activity, the consciousness of doing good, peace of mind and a bright hope of glorious destiny hereafter? Away with the word in such a view and with such a thought! It is emphatically no sacrifice. Say rather it is a privilege."

In the early 20th century, some pioneer missionaries were holding an evangelistic outreach in the backwaters of Togo, West Africa. On the first night of their preaching, a destitute peasant woman was powerfully impacted and decided to surrender her life to Christ. As was the cultural custom, each subsequent evening those touched by the message would bring gifts of yam or maize and lay them on the altar at the front in gratitude to God. This particular woman was so poor that she had nothing to bring each evening, although she desperately longed to show how grateful she was. However, on the last night of the week's outreach, she came forward in the throng and triumphantly placed a silver coin on the altar. It was worth a dollar, which was a significant sum in those days. The missionary in charge saw her and feared that she had stolen it; but he didn't want her to lose face in public. So he waited until after the meeting had finished before he approached her and asked her how she could have afforded such a lavish gift. Eyes beaming, she replied that she was so happy to be free from her crippling guilt, to know where she was headed, and to discover the depth of the love Jesus had for her, that she wanted to contribute to making Jesus known to others who hadn't yet heard. She had considered it a privilege to go to a nearby plantation owner and sell herself as a slave for life for one dollar. That was the gift she laid on the altar that night.

Through the centuries and through the generations, thousands of people have chosen to lay their lives down on the altar in total surrender. May we likewise be willing to pay the ultimate price. A while back I wrote in my journal: "Lord, thank you so much for choosing me. What an incredible adventure is the life of faith! You could have allowed me to opt for an easier life, but what richness and depths of emotion and experience would have been missed out on. Do I envy what the world has to offer, which so many are enticed by? I answer a resounding *'No!'* You are worth everything, and I gladly surrender it all to you. I bless your glorious name for the privilege of being your child. Conform me ever-increasingly to your likeness. For your name's sake. Amen!"

So What's it Worth?

At your feet I fall,
Yield you up my all,
To suffer, live, or die
For my Lord crucified.

L. B. Cowman

The kingdom of heaven is like treasure hidden in a field. When a man found it, he hid it again, and then in his joy went and sold all he had and bought that field. Again, the kingdom of heaven is like a merchant looking for fine pearls. When he found one of great value, he went away and sold everything he had and bought it.

Matthew 13:44–46

So what's it worth to follow Jesus all the way? In the above short parables, Jesus is showing how reasonable it is to give up everything in order to purchase the field with the hidden treasure in it, or the fine pearl. The merchant, or businessman, realizes the incredible worth of the discovery he has made, and urgently tries to lay hold of it as soon as possible at whatever cost. Clearly he's not agonizing over the price – no, he knows that what he's discovered is of such immeasurable value that, however long it takes, whatever the effort, whatever the cost, it will be worth it. Consequently his worry isn't the sacrifice he'll have to make to get it, but rather whether someone else will get there first and he'll miss out on such a life-transforming and life-enhancing gift. He does it joyfully, knowing he has more than hit the jackpot. What's it worth? Anything and everything.

Mrs Shirley Martin went to the local Salvation Army thrift store in Vancouver and bought a box of buttons for one dollar. Her husband, a postman, was fast asleep one evening as she rummaged through the box. Amongst the many buttons, something sparkled. It looked like a diamond. She rushed through to the bedroom and woke her husband. "Darling, I think I've found a diamond!"

"Oh, come on, dear, you're always having these crazy ideas," he replied, and nodded off again.

Mrs Martin took the gem to twelve different jewellers. Some dismissed it as junk (one said it was worth 49 cents!), but others shook when they held it. Gemologist Hans Reymer appraised the gem at $19,300. Mrs Martin had accidentally come across a precious stone for just one dollar!

However wonderful that chance discovery was for Mrs Martin, there's an infinitely more precious stone on offer to us. It's the Pearl of Great Price. Some may think it's a load of junk and dismiss it. Others (even those very close to us) may think that it's just another "crazy idea". But if we know the true value of the Pearl, then we won't give up because of what others say; rather we'll pursue it and do anything and everything to appropriate it.

The exciting thing about deciding to follow Jesus is that he drops a pearl of great price into each of our box of buttons, similar to what happened with Mrs Martin. It's a gift. It's a gift of grace. We haven't earned it; but we're responsible for recognizing its worth, and for what we do with it. Like Mrs Martin, we're just one of billions of people on this planet going about our daily business. And our lives can be very humdrum and seemingly insignificant until we stumble across this extraordinary treasure. But from that point on, our lives are never the same again.

The Caller is calling. What will he do with you and me? If you imagine a plain bar of iron worth just £10, it could be turned into a number of different things: maybe into a pair of horseshoes worth £100, or a box of sewing needles worth £10,000, or a case of balance springs for fine Swiss watches worth £1,000,000. The raw material was just a plain bar of iron – but what a difference in eventual worth! God, do whatever you want with me! You're the Giver, and you give more talents to some than to others. That's your call. But may I not settle for a horseshoe when I could be so much more! Have your way in my life!

"Not by might nor by power, but by my Spirit"

God wants to use us to change the world. The combined onslaught of secular humanism and Islam seems to be forcing the church into beating a hasty retreat. Yet God's people have weathered numerous crises and storms through three millennia, and we'll do so again. The prophet Zechariah wrote in the sixth century BC, "'Not by might nor by power, but by my Spirit,' says the Lord Almighty" (Zechariah 4:6). At the time, the Israelites were in exile, dejected and downcast. But the Babylonian empire was coming to its end, and the prophet Isaiah's call rang out to rebuild Jerusalem and Israel as a whole. His unenviable task was to re-envision his despairing compatriots to embark by foot on the arduous thousand-mile trek back to their destroyed homeland. All indicators suggested it was a hopeless dream. Could

Jerusalem really be transformed? Could the temple really be rebuilt? Could morale really be restored? Well, although it took longer than anyone might have imagined, the impossible happened. Zechariah's words proved true: "'Not by might nor by power, but by my Spirit,' says the Lord Almighty."

Throughout history God has used different tools to cause his church to return to him, to grow or to spread. Sometimes it was foreign powers, other times foreign ideologies or belief systems. In the early church he used persecution. And as more and more religiously intolerant legislation is advocated in our land nowadays, maybe a period of suffering and persecution will be his chosen tool to refine and define a new generation of Christians who are willing to lay their lives down for their King. However our upcoming trials manifest themselves, we can choose to see them as opportunities instead of problems. Hurdles can become launching pads, stumbling blocks can become stepping stones, apparent setbacks can blow wide open new avenues of potential service, failures can be transformed into triumphs. Why? Because as Jesus demonstrated, death was the precursor to resurrection.

As with those exiles in Babylon, we need to repent and return to God. We need to renew our commitment to our Father, to his Son, to his Holy Spirit, to his Word. Mahatma Gandhi commented to a group of missionaries about their treatment of the Bible, "You Christians look after a document containing enough dynamite to blow all civilization to pieces, turn the world upside down and bring peace to a battle-torn planet. But you treat it as though it is nothing more than a piece of literature." So we choose to get back to the Book, and see it as far more than a piece of literature or a text book, but as containing an explosive and dynamic message with power to transform cultures, institutions, regimes and civilizations. Beyond that, we recognize that the world doesn't need text books about Jesus but text people whose lives proclaim loud and clear that Jesus is the way, the truth and the life.

To do that, we're given the power of the Holy Spirit. So we call on him to turn the world upside down, starting with you and me. We embrace whatever and however he chooses to operate, even if it's not how we would have envisaged it. Catherine Fox wrote, "The Biblical images to describe the work of the Spirit – fire, mighty rushing wind, flood etc. – are exactly the sorts of things we pay to insure ourselves against." It's perhaps a daunting prospect, as we accept his leadership and authority over our lives. But William Temple warned us that "if we invoke the Holy Spirit, we must be ready for the glorious pain of being caught by his power [and taken] out of our petty orbit into the eternal purposes of the Almighty".

Not going alone

The challenge excites me. Just as the Holy Spirit laid hold of a ragtag bunch of disillusioned and confused disciples, and transformed them into fearless impassioned messengers of grace, so he can lay hold of you and me in the same way. We could be on the edge of something far bigger and more significant and powerful than our minds can conceive – because that's exactly what the Holy Spirit is like. Foster writes,

In our day heaven and earth are on tiptoe waiting for the emerging of a Spirit-led, Spirit-intoxicated, Spirit-empowered people. All of creation watches expectantly for the springing up of a disciplined, freely gathered, martyr people who know in this life the life and power of the kingdom of God. It has happened before. It can happen again... Such a people will not emerge until there is among us a deeper, more profound experience of an Emmanuel of the Spirit – God with us, a knowledge that in the power of the Spirit Jesus has come to guide his people himself, an experience of his leading that is as definite and as immediate as the cloud by day and fire by night.

Yes, I'm excited. And we've come full circle. At the very beginning of this book, the stated aim was to contribute to the reclaiming of a dynamic, thoughtful, cutting-edge and relevant gospel to raise the bar and arrest the decline of both the quality and quantity of those who purport to follow the Lord Jesus Christ in the Western world. However, it's become abundantly clear through these pages that putting it all into practice won't be easy. In fact, it will be a real struggle. The enemy will fight it all the way, because he knows the powerful witness it will be to the kingdom-of-God-among-us. Few will understand, even within the Body of Christ. We can't expect non-believers to understand, but it hurts to be the brunt of the disapprobation of fellow brothers and sisters who have decided, consciously or unwittingly, to reject the radical call to follow in the footsteps of the Master.

As we set out to live passionately for Jesus, it will be helpful for us to embark on the adventure with other fellow travellers. It's a lonely road on our own, but in a group of like-minded people, who share the vision and embrace the ideals, the journey will be more fun. There's always strength and solidarity in numbers. As an African proverb says, "If you want to go fast, go alone. But if you want to go far, go together." We want to go far, so it will help to go together. You may struggle to find many people on the same wavelength, but in most churches there are at least a handful of like-minded enthusiasts who are itching for a deeper reality and primal rawness in their spiritual journey. Team up, pray together, live together, share your lives together. Be "iron sharpening iron", challenging and spurring each other on to dreaming dreams and acting them out. Get stuck in together, fleshing out your faith as Jesus' hands and feet in an effective, coordinated and strategic way wherever you're called to be.

I'm not advocating anything new. It's been done plenty of times before throughout history. In 564 AD, for example, Saint Columba set sail with twelve disciples. They were a tight-knit band of Jesus radicals, whose dreams were earthed in their conviction that God works most powerfully through small faithful bands of intimate disciples, grittily living together and sharing their lives in open vulnerability. They didn't know their destination, but they trusted that in leaving their native Ireland, they would be guided to wherever God wanted them to serve him. God duly led them to a small island just off Scotland, where they founded what they described as a "little heavenly community" called Iona.

The prevailing culture all around them was pagan, but they weren't the types to settle for sanctified resignation as they observed the dark world they found themselves in. They were on a mission from God! But their approach was totally unlike the church in Rome, whose top-down system was becoming progressively more hierarchical and institutionalized, and whose unwieldy centralized structures sucked the spiritual lifeblood out of most of those who claimed to follow Jesus. In complete contrast, these Jesus radicals sought to ferment their ideals and spirituality from the grassroots of society upwards.

In due course, Columba reached out to the bloodthirsty Picts in northern Scotland, and eventually led the king of the Picts to Christ. Steadily the missionary forays from the community at Iona permeated much of Scotland, and then England, and even mainland Europe. Wherever they went, they established new "little heavenly communities" as beacons of light and life to reach out to the lost souls around them. This surging vibrant movement's manual was the book of Acts, and the results weren't dissimilar to those achieved by the early church.

Can we relearn some lessons from Columba and his merry men? Their commitment to each other and to reaching the lost was total. Their servant-hearted faith was lived out in uncluttered simplicity. Their bold, risk-taking and adventurous spirit was unquenchable. And the bedrock of it all was their passionate love for Jesus. So like them, I want to fall in love with Jesus again. Thomas Aquinas was one of the world's greatest ever theologians. He stopped writing one day, although he still had plenty of wisdom to impart to future generations across the centuries. His secretary remonstrated with him, insisting he continue. But Thomas replied, "Brother Reginald, when I was at prayer a few months ago, I experienced something of the reality of Jesus Christ. That day, I lost all appetite for writing. In fact, all I have ever written about Christ seems now to me to be like straw." I pray for a fresh and ever-deepening experience of the reality of Jesus Christ. If that's to happen, Chambers counsels us to "get alone with Jesus and either tell him that you don't want sin to die out in you; or else tell him that at all costs you want to be identified with his death".

Join the fellowship of the unashamed

As we've already said, few may be called upon to die for their faith, but identifying with Jesus' death will involve getting to such a place of willingness to do so. If we're accused of being alarmist or extremist, it will be by those with no comprehension of the battle raging around us for the hearts, minds and souls of a lost humanity. There will be casualties, but the cause we fight for warrants the cost. One Zimbabwean young man wrote the following before he was martyred: "I'm part of the fellowship of the unashamed. I have the Holy Spirit's power. The die has been cast. I've stepped over the line. The decision has been made – I'm a disciple of his. I won't look back, let up, slow down, back away, or be still... I will not flinch in the face of sacrifice, hesitate in the presence of the enemy, pander at the pool of popularity, or meander in the maze of mediocrity... I am a disciple of Jesus. I must go till he comes, give till I drop, preach till all know, and work till he stops me. And, when he comes for his own, he will have no problem recognizing me... my banner will be clear!"

In stark contrast, let's make sure we don't get to the end of our lives and resonate with the following poem:

To sinful patterns of behaviour that never get confronted
    and changed,
Abilities and gifts that never get cultivated and deployed –
Until weeks become months
And months turn into years,
And one day you're looking back on a life of
Deep intimate gut-wrenchingly honest conversations
    you never had;
Great bold prayers you never prayed,
Exhilarating risks you never took,
Sacrificial gifts you never offered,
Lives you never touched,
And you're sitting in a recliner with a shriveled soul.
And forgotten dreams,
And you realise there was a world of desperate need,
And a great God calling you to be part of something
    bigger than yourself –
You see the person you could have become but did not;
You never followed your calling.
You never got out of the boat.

So join forces in the fellowship of the unashamed, covenant together, jump out of the boat, and wade into the deep, safe in the knowledge that Jesus is there. Embrace the uncertainty and adventure of the next exciting chapter in your life, which will be... God knows what, God knows where, God knows when, God knows with whom, and God knows how. He knows the answers. You may or may not. That's why we live by faith. That's the call to no holds barred discipleship. And that's what he's worth. Are you up for the challenge? Bring it on!

Bibliography

ACUTE, *The Nature of Hell: A Report by the Evangelical Alliance Commission on Unity and Truth Among Evangelicals*, Paternoster, Carlisle, 2000

Dietrich Bonhoeffer, *The Cost of Discipleship*, Broadman & Holman, Nashville, TN, 1999

Bread for the World Institute, *What Governments Can Do: Hunger 1997*, Silver Spring, MD, 1996

Brother Andrew and Al Janssen, *Light Force*, Hodder & Stoughton, London, 2004

Jerry Bridges, *The Pursuit of Holiness*, NavPress, Colorado Springs, CO, 1996

Alex Buchanan, *Heaven and Hell*, Sovereign World, Tonbridge, 1995

Tony Campolo, *Let Me Tell you a Story*, Word Publishing, Nashville, TN, 2000

Amy Carmichael, "Thy Brother's Blood Crieth" from *Things as They Are*, Dohnavur Fellowship, India, 1921

E. G. Carré (ed.), *Praying Hyde: Apostle of Prayer*, Bridge-Logos, Gainesville, FL, 2004

Oswald Chambers, *My Utmost for His Highest*, Barbour Books, Uhrichsville, OH, 1987

Oswald Chambers, *So Send I You/Workmen of God: Recognizing and Answering God's Call to Service*, Discovery House, Uhrichsville, OH, 1987

L. B. Cowman, *Streams in the Desert*, Cowman Publications, 1925, Zondervan, Grand Rapids, MI, 1997

Eileen Crossman, *Mountain Rain*, Paternoster Lifestyle, Carlisle, 2001

Brent Curtis and John Eldredge, *The Sacred Romance: Drawing Closer to the Heart of God*, Thomas Nelson, Nashville, TN, 1997

Anthony De Mello, *The Song of the Bird*, Gujaret Sahitya Prakash, Anand, India, distributed by Loyola University Press, Chicago, IL, 1983

Jonathan Edwards, *On Knowing Christ*, Banner of Truth Trust, Edinburgh, 1990

Jonathan Edwards, *The Life of David Brainerd*, Norman Pettit (ed.), *The Works of Jonathan Edwards*, Vol. 7, Yale University Press, New Haven, CT, 1985

John Eldredge, *Wild at Heart: Discovering the Secret of a Man's Soul*, Thomas Nelson, Nashville, TN, 2001

John Eldredge, *Waking the Dead: The Glory of a Heart Fully Alive*, Thomas Nelson, Nashville, TN, 2003

Steve Farrar, *Finishing Strong: Going the Distance for your Family*, Multnomah Press, Sisters, OR, 1995

Richard Foster, *Prayer: Finding the Heart's True Home*, HarperSanFrancisco, 1992

Great Commission Roundtable, Port Dickson, Malaysia, April–May 2001

Mark Greene, *Thank God it's Monday: Ministry in the Workplace*, Scripture Union, Bletchley, 1994

Pete Greig, *The Vision and the Vow*, Relevant Media, Lake Mary, FL, 2004

Os Guinness, *The Call*, Word Publishing, Nashville, TN, 1998

Ole Hallesby, *Prayer*, Augsburg, Minneapolis, MN, 1994

Nicholas Herman, alias Brother Lawrence, *The Practice of the Presence of God*, Fleming H. Revell, Old Tapan, NJ, 1974

Clifford Hill, *The Wilberforce Connection*, Monarch Books, Oxford, 2005

R. Kent Hughes, *1001 Great Stories & Quotes*, Tyndale House Publishers, inc., Wheaton, Illinois, 1998

Walter B. Knight, *Knight's Master Book of New Illustrations*, Eerdmans, Grand Rapids, MI, 1956

C. S. Lewis, *Mere Christianity*, Macmillan, New York, 1967

C. S. Lewis, *The Last Battle*, Collier, New York, 1970

C. S. Lewis, *The Great Divorce*, Fontana, Glasgow, 1972

Brennan Manning, *Signature of Jesus*, Multnomah Press, Sisters, OR, 1996

Brennan Manning, *The Ragamuffin Gospel*, Multnomah Press, Sisters, OR, 1999

Erwin Raphael McManus, *The Barbarian Way*, Thomas Nelson, Nashville, TN, 2005

Thomas Merton, *Contemplative Prayer*, Darton, Longman & Todd, London, 2005

Andrew Murray, *Key to the Missionary Problem*, Christian Literature Crusade, Fort Washington, PA, 1979

John Ortberg, *If You Want to Walk on Water, You've Got to Get Out of the Boat*, Zondervan, Grand Rapids, MI, 2001

John Ortberg, *The Life You've Always Wanted*, Zondervan, Grand Rapids, MI, 2002

Ross Paterson, *What in the World is God Waiting For?*, Sovereign World, Tonbridge, 2005, formerly published as *The Antioch Factor*, 2000

James Paton (ed.), *John G. Paton: Missionary to the New Hebrides, An Autobiography*, Banner of Truth Trust, London, 1965, originally 1891

David Pawson, *The Road to Hell*, Hodder and Stoughton, Sevenoaks, 1992

Scott Peck, *The Different Drum*, Simon & Schuster, New York, 1987

Clark H. Pinnock, "An Evangelical Theology of Human Liberation", *Sojourners*, February 1976

John Piper, *Let the Nations be Glad*, Baker Books, Grand Rapids, MI, 1993

Ewald Plass (ed.), *What Luther Says*, 3 vols., Concordia, St Louis, 1959

Vaughan Roberts, *Distinctives*, Authentic Lifestyle, Milton Keynes, 2000

Francis A. Schaeffer, *The Church at the End of the Twentieth Century*, Inter-Varsity Press, Downers Grove, IL, 1970

Ronald Sider, *Rich Christians in an Age of Hunger*, Hodder and Stoughton, Sevenoaks, 1997

George Smith, *Life of William Carey, Shoemaker and Missionary*, 1909, reprinted 1913

Paul D. Stanley and J. Robert Clinton, *Connecting: The Mentoring Relationships You Need to Succeed in Life*, NavPress, Colorado Springs, CO, 1992

Roger Steer, *Delighted in God*, Hodder & Stoughton, London, 1981

A. W. Tozer, *The Pursuit of God: The Human Thirst for the Divine*, Christian Publications, 1982

A. W. Tozer, *The Knowledge of the Holy*, Authentic Media, Milton Keynes, 2005

Jean Watson, *Through the Year with David Watson*, Hodder & Stoughton, Sevenoaks, 1982

Dallas Willard, *The Divine Conspiracy*, HarperSanFrancisco, 1998

Philip Yancey, *Soul Survivor: How My Faith Survived the Church*, Hodder & Stoughton, London, 2003

Samuel Young, *Giving and Living*, Baker Books, Grand Rapids, 1984

John Zumwalt, *Gospel According to John*, (Heart of God Ministries, Oklahoma)

Great Lakes Outreach

A few years ago, I set up Great Lakes Outreach (GLO), a UK charity (reg. no. 4686283) which works in partnership with several organisations in the Great Lakes region of Central Africa, notably in Burundi. Its purpose is to respond to the area's massive needs and the huge potential impact of strategic involvement in cooperation with key Burundian partners.

The main areas of GLO's involvement include:

• Evangelism and discipleship through schools and churches

• Printing of teaching materials

• Fighting the AIDS pandemic

• Supporting a street children's project

• Helping to sustain an orphanage

• Equipping and encouraging informed dialogue between Christians and Muslims

• Training university students in outreach

• Small business development opportunities to enable income-generation and self-sustainability

All proceeds from the sale of this book will go to the work of GLO. I would love you to get involved in what the Lord is doing out in Burundi, so do get in touch by contacting info@greatlakesoutreach.org or visit our website: www.greatlakesoutreach.org There are opportunities to come out on short-term teams, to contribute financially, to become a regional representative, and to subscribe for more detailed and personal prayer information. I look forward to hearing from you.